Make Your Life
Tax Deductible

Make Your Life Tax Deductible

David W. Meier

McGraw-Hill

New York   Chicago   San Francisco   Lisbon   London
Madrid   Mexico City   Milan   New Delhi   San Juan
Seoul   Singapore   Sydney   Toronto

Copyright © 2006 by The Meier Institutes, Inc. All rights reserved. Printed in the United States of America. Except as permitted under the United States Copyright Act of 1976, no part of this publication may be reproduced or distributed in any form or by any means, or stored in a data base or retrieval system, without the prior written permission of the publisher.

 3 4 5 6 7 8 9 0   AGM/AGM   0 9 8

ISBN 0-07-146762-9

This publication is designed to provide accurate and authoritative information in regard to the subject matter covered. It is sold with the understanding that the publisher is not engaged in rendering legal, accounting, or other professional service. If legal advice or other expert assistance is required, the services of a competent professional person should be sought.
—*From a Declaration of Principles jointly adopted by a Committee of the American Bar Association and a Committee of Publishers and Associations*

McGraw-Hill books are available at special quantity discounts to use as premiums and sales promotions, or for use in corporate training programs. For more information, please write to the Director of Special Sales, Professional Publishing, McGraw-Hill, Two Penn Plaza, New York, NY 10121-2298. Or contact your local bookstore.

Library of Congress Cataloging-in-Publication Data

Meier, David W.
  Make your life tax deductible : easy techniques to reduce your taxes and start building wealth immediately—from America's number one small business tax authority / David W. Meier.
    p. cm.
  Includes index.
  ISBN 0-07-146762-9 (alk. paper)
  1. Small business—Taxation—United States.   2. Small business—Taxation—Law and legislation—United States.
  3. Self-employed—United States.   4. Sole proprietorship.   5. Small business—Management.   I. Title.
  HD2346.U5M45 2006
  658.15'92—dc22   2005025265

In loving memory of my mother,
Betty May Meier,
and my father,
Weston Alger Meier,
who encouraged and helped me
every step along the way
with their unconditional love.

Contents

Table of Tax Strategies

Part 2. Your Persona

Part 3. Your Retirement

Acknowledgments

I have constantly been uplifted by my brother's accomplishments and ongoing successes—which are achieved against all odds . . . thanks, Ricky.

Over the years, I've needed someone who, because they believe in me, is always there to encourage me, to help pave the way, and to be my best friend . . . thanks, Bob.

My successes are so much more enjoyable when shared with my family; and my challenges are much more tolerable because my family offers a safe haven of love and understanding . . . thanks, Arlene and Chris.

For one whose IRS experience, insight, and friendship I have relied on for well over a decade . . . thanks, Shirley.

It's great to have someone who believes in my work as much as I do . . . thanks, Mike.

My accomplishments are not just for me, but are also for my son, the most important person in my life . . . thanks, Jeremy.

Make Your Life Tax Deductible

How to Make Your Life Tax Deductible

It's important for you to keep in mind that taxes are neither fair nor logical, and this becomes painfully obvious the more you learn about the Tax Code and the role of the Internal Revenue Service (IRS). Furthermore, IRS Tax Code is subject to change at a moment's notice. The United States Congress approves taxing concepts; then the IRS is responsible for writing the Tax Code, which is the set of rules and regulations (in the form of tax law) detailing the specific rules that all tax payers must follow in the preparation, filing, and paying of their taxes. Then the U.S. Congress passes tax law reflecting the Tax Code created by the IRS. The IRS is empowered to administer and enforce all federal income tax laws and to collect all pertinent taxes.

It's very difficult (and for the most part a complete waste of *your* time) for you to dive into the IRS Tax Code in an effort to understand all the details and to stay current with all the changes. Fortunately, I've already done that for you. All you are required to do is read and apply the strategies and information in this book, all of which have been developed to allow you to take advantage of the very favorable tax laws applicable to small-business ownership, to truly make your life tax deductible!

The rationale behind the IRS and Congress using tax law to engage in social engineering regarding small-business owners (creating tax law that leads small-business taxpayers to take actions that are good for the economy as a whole) is that it is becoming evident that the future success of the U.S. economy is increasingly dependent on the growth of small businesses. For example, it is estimated that upward to 60 percent of the future growth in jobs will be directly attributable to small businesses—their creation and subsequent growth. Therefore, it's beneficial for the economy to give breaks to these small businesses that will allow them to succeed.

In the final analysis, it's up to you! Small business owners enjoy two distinct benefits: (1) the profit that the businesses generate (profit that is under the control of the business owners and can be used as they see fit) and (2) tremendous tax savings (the opportunity to convert personal expenditures into tax-deductible expenses and thus to enjoy considerable tax savings). Remember, you can enjoy profits and tax savings no matter what size your business is; small businesses are just as able to generate both profits and tax savings as larger businesses.

The goal in applying small-business tax strategies is to match all the allowable business tax deductions of your business against the taxable (gross) income of the business. In this manner you will minimize its taxable income.

If you work for someone as an employee, the income you generate (in the form of W-2 wages) is subject to income taxes. This means that before you can spend any of these dollars, you must first pay all federal and state (if applicable) income taxes due. The tax due can amount to tens of thousands of dollars—drastically reducing the after-tax dollars you have available for your personal use.

However, when you become a small business owner, tax law turns in your favor. You no longer have to pay taxes first, before you spend the profit your small business generates. Before you calculate any taxes due on business profit, you may first deduct the dollar amount of any and all "ordinary and necessary" expenditures that your business has incurred (in pursuit of profit). Although these tax-deductible expenditures must be related to your business, you'll soon find that many personal expenditures—for travel, cars, home, and even entertainment—become tax-deductible business expenses. As a small business owner, you can literally *make your life tax deductible*. This book shows you how it works!

STRATEGY 1

Take advantage of the tremendous tax savings available to you directly as a result of owning your own business.

As an individual (nonbusiness) taxpayer, your federal marginal income tax rate will be anywhere from 10 to 35 percent of all the income that you earn. Your goal should always be to maximize your tax deductions in order to minimize your taxable income, and therefore to minimize your income tax due.

As an individual (nonbusiness) taxpayer, the number and dollar amount of potential tax deductions is severely limited. When you own your own business, however, you literally have the opportunity to make your *life* tax deductible. This means that the items you paid for out of after-tax dollars (i.e., after paying any taxes due) as a nonbusiness owner, you can now pay out of pretax dollars (i.e., before paying any taxes due)—thus drastically reducing your taxable income and therefore your total income tax liability.

The marginal income tax rate applicable to your particular business is a function of your form of business organization and the annual dollar amount of profit your business generates, matters discussed throughout this book. For now, though, keep in mind that this rate can vary from 10 percent at the low end to a maximum of 39 percent. (Depending on your business's form of organization, there may be an additional 15.3 percent due, on top of the 28 percent tax rate, for self-employment tax.) Let's assume for the sake of the following example, that your business's federal marginal income tax rate is 28 percent.

As a business owner, you are entitled to deduct a much broader range of items than you did as an individual taxpayer. Business tax deductions, created by the Internal Revenue Service (IRS), enable you to deduct the cost of items that would otherwise not be tax deductible to you as an individual taxpayer, including the following:

• Your home
• Your car
• Your equipment
• Your travel and entertainment
• Your family and yourself
• Your strategic issues
• Your retirement

These business-related expenses can generate a substantial dollar amount of tax deductions for you each and every tax year. Let's assume that for a given tax year the preceding items generated tax deductions totaling $90,000 (a very conservative number, given the potential tax deductions available to you as a business owner). This $90,000 in tax deductions generates just over $25,000 in tax savings ($90,000 × 28%). If the tax rate applicable to your business profit is 39 percent, the applicable tax savings would be just over $35,000 ($90,000 × 39%).

You can now ask yourself, "Is there something I would like to do with this $25,000 to $35,000 in additional cash? Would I like to spend more money on my family? Maybe I would prefer to save more for my family's future and for my retirement." Whatever use you put these additional dollars to, it would certainly be far better than paying that money to the IRS.

It's possible, as a business owner, to generate significant savings for yourself and your family with business-related tax deductions. When you "make your life tax deductible," you reap significant additional dollars to do with as you wish.

STRATEGY 2

Understand and apply the tremendous latitude that you are allowed, as a small business owner, in taking full advantage of the IRS's many business tax deductions.

The only requirement in order to make your life tax deductible is that you own your own business. Your ability to own your own business—one that generates tax savings for you (personally)—is not limited by such factors as (1) the size of your business, (2) the time you spend in your business, (3) the business's location, or (4) its profitability. In fact, you are allowed a great deal of latitude in setting up and operating your business. Consider the following:

1. *The size of your business.* Your business could be large, with thousands of dollars in sales revenue and many employees; or it could be one that generates small dollar sales with few or no employees (except yourself); or it could be somewhere in between.
2. *The time you spend in your business.* Whether you work full-time or part-time in your business, all the tax deductions and tax savings are available to you.
3. *The business's location.* Your business could have a significant physical plant or a large retail storefront; or you could run the business out of your home; or it could be run both outside and inside your home.
4. *Its profitability.* If your business is profitable (for any given tax year), the tax deductions that are created by making your life tax deductible will create tax savings to your business. Even if the business is not profitable (either in the beginning or for any given tax year), this loss may be passed along to your personal individual 1040 tax return (depending on your form of business organization) and used to offset your other income (such as W-2 wages) for the year.

STRATEGY 3

Minimize your business's income tax liability by deducting all applicable "ordinary and necessary" business expenses.

Ordinary and necessary business deductions, or *common operating expenses* (as they are sometimes called), include all the expenses required to operate your business. These deductions are not particularly difficult to understand, nor do they require any special knowledge to implement properly; however, some do require the application of specific tax strategies to maximize the tax advantage. Some ordinary and necessary expenses vary from business to business; however, most of them are deductible without regard to your business type.

Business expenses that are considered "ordinary and necessary" to a small business fall into two distinct categories: (1) those that are *expensed*, meaning that the entire cost of the item is deducted (expensed) in the year in which it is incurred, and (2) those that are *capitalized*, meaning that the entire cost of the item is deducted (expensed) over its theoretical useful life (as determined by the IRS). Following are specific examples of "ordinary and necessary" small-business expenses.

STRATEGY 4

Expense the cost of expenditures your business makes for items with a useful life less than one year.

Those that are expensed include:

- Professional services: accounting, attorney, consultant
- Logistical support: alarm services; online services; dues and subscriptions; rent, cleaning, utilities, telephone; office supplies; postage, freight, and shipping; printing; repairs and maintenance
- Financial: bank service charges, interest expense, and other fees
- Office expenses (outside rent, home office expenses, etc.)
- Travel
- Your car

  Your business can take the number of business miles driven using a specific car multiplied by 40.5 cents per mile, and you can do so every year.

  Your business can deduct all the actual expenses of owning and operating a specific car for business purposes. (Note: The actual cost of the car is deducted under capitalized expenditures.)

- Entertainment
- Retirement funding
- Hiring your family
- Tax-free owner benefits (company cars, long-term care, life insurance, etc.)
- Wages and salaries
- Retirement plan contributions
- Employee benefits (child care, education, adoption)
- Marketing
- Business insurance
- Medical health insurance (for the business owner(s) and employees)
- Payroll taxes
- Other taxes (e.g., sales taxes)
- Start-up and organizational expenditures incurred after October 22, 2004 (under $5000)

STRATEGY 5

Capitalize **the cost of expenditures your business makes for items with a useful life greater than one year.**

Those that are capitalized include:

- Your car (the actual cost of your car, applicable to business use, is deducted over five (5) years using depreciation methods, bonus depreciation, and "Section 179"
- Equipment, furniture, and fixtures (deducted over seven years)
- Real estate (deducted over five years)
- Start-up and organizational expenditures (in excess of $5000)*

---

*Start-up and organizational expenses include costs that are incurred by your business prior to the day it begins actual business operations; they end when your business actively begins to offer its products or services to potential customers. These expenses include such business costs as licensing fees, incorporation fees (plus the cost of creating stock certificates and the corporate minutes book), and the cost of acquiring consulting services (prior to beginning operations). Total expenditures are deducted over a 60-month time period, beginning when your business actually makes its products/services available for purchase.

This book discusses both expensed and capitalized deductions, but first, let's examine some big-picture tax strategies for your small business.

STRATEGY 6

Allocate expenditures between personal and business.

An expenditure does not have to be either entirely tax deductible or nondeductible. You must allocate expenditures between personal and business use. The personal portion is not tax deductible; however, the business part is usually tax deductible as a business expense. An example of this would be staying in a hotel for six nights when only four days were required for business purposes. The remaining two were for personal use and therefore not deductible. If you are prorating expenditures that do not divide as easily between personal and business use, you can elect to deduct the appropriate business-related percentage, which is calculated by determining the portion of your activity that could be considered business. For example, you can use number of days considered business days as a percentage of the total days of the activity (e.g., four business-related nights divided by six total nights equals 66.67 percent), and then apply that percentage to, for example, your total rental car expenditures for the six days. Similarly, four days of a car rental applicable to business would be deductible and two days for personal use would not.

STRATEGY 7

Avoid the IRS's "hobby rule."

You are presumed by the IRS to be "in business" with the intent to make a profit if you show a profit in three out of five years. You may be required to demonstrate and defend the fact that you are operating with the genuine intent of making a profit. It is generally rather easy to prove by showing that your business has the capability to provide products and services to potential customers and that it is making significant marketing efforts; and it is further demonstrated by the nature of the business you're in. For example, it's much easier to make a case for being "in business in pursuit of profit" when you're in the consulting business, as opposed to the cat-raising business. Even so, you're better off if you never have to prove anything to the IRS. For that reason alone, you should manage your activity with the idea of creating profit. Furthermore, if your business is not profitable, why are you still in that business, anyway? If you don't meet this criterion and the IRS determines your business to be a "hobby," you are allowed deductions only up to the extent of income. Therefore, you cannot show a loss should you incur one. Going back to previous tax years, the IRS will disallow deductions that were taken in excess of the income from the activity.

STRATEGY 8

Estimate your business's income tax liability as a function of its form of organization and its estimated annual profit.

Your *marginal income tax rate* is the tax rate applicable to the next dollar of profit your business generates. By knowing your marginal income tax rate, you will know how much tax you will have to pay on every additional dollar over and above your current taxable income. By creating tax deductions, you can significantly reduce your taxable income, and in the process you also could reduce your marginal income tax rate.

The lower your marginal income tax rate, the higher your proportionate after-tax income, and therefore the more of your income you will be able to keep.

Depending on the form of business organization you select for your business, your business's taxable income will be subject to your own federal personal marginal income tax rate or corporate marginal income tax rates. This book discusses the various forms of business organizations in depth in Part 1. If your form of business organization is either a sole proprietorship, a partnership, a limited partnership, a one-member limited liability company (LLC-1) taxed as a sole proprietorship or an S corporation, a multiple-member limited liability company (LLC), or an S corporation, your business's taxable income will be subject to your federal personal marginal income tax rates of 10 to 35 percent. (See Table I.1, "Federal Personal Income Tax Rates.")

If your form of business organization is either a one-member limited liability company (LLC-1) taxed as a C corporation, a multiple-member limited liability company (LLC) taxed as a C corporation, or an actual C corporation, your business's taxable

Table I.1   Federal Personal Income Tax Rates

Based on Taxable Income

Single	Married Filing Jointly	Federal Tax Rate
Not over $7,000	Not over $14,000	10%
Over $7,000–$28,400	Over $14,000–$56,800	15%
Over $28,400–$68,800	Over $56,800–$114,650	25%
Over $68,800–$143,500	Over $114,650–$174,700	28%
Over $143,500–$311,950	Over $174,700–$311,950	33%
Over $311,950	Over $311,950	35%

income will be subject to federal corporate marginal income tax rates of 15 to 39 percent. (See Table I.2, "Federal Corporation Income Tax Rates.")

The range of income tax rates applicable to businesses is also a function of the amount of profit your business is expected to generate. Obviously, the greater the amount of profit, the higher the applicable tax rate. Therefore, the tax rate that will apply to your business is a function of both its form of organization and the dollar amount of expected annual profit.

Table I.2   Federal Corporation Income Tax Rates

Based on Taxable Income

Taxable Income	Tax Rate
$0–$50,000	15%
$50,001–75,000	25%
$75,001–$100,000	34%
$100,001–$335,000	39%
$335,001–$10,000,000	34%
$10,000,001–$15,000,000	35%
$15,000,001–$18,333,333	38%
$18,333,334 and higher	35%

How to Use This Book

To make it as easy as possible for you to make your life tax deductible, this book is arranged in an easy-to-access format. You'll find more than 150 deductions in Parts 1, 2, and 3.

- Part 1 includes information and strategies pertaining to the form of your organization. The advantages and disadvantages of the major forms of business organization that are available to business owners are discussed. Included are specific strategies designed to help you decide what form of business organization is best for your business. Part 1 will help you decide on a form of organization that will minimize your business's income tax liability.
- Part 2 covers each of the major ways you can convert personal expenditures into tax-deductible business expenses. The information and strategies in Part 2 focus on such items as your home, your car, and other personal expenditures that can also have a business purpose. Once you have chosen the form of business organization that minimizes taxes, "Your Persona" helps you further minimize your business's income tax liability by addressing these issues.
- Part 3 explains retirement planning, one of the most significant (if not *the* most significant) ways that business owners can further reduce their business income tax liability while at the same time beginning the process of accumulating and growing their personal wealth. You'll learn strategies for establishing and funding your own retirement plan—sponsored by your own business. The information offered in "Your Retirement" is arguably the most powerful way you can accumulate substantial wealth, and to do so either tax-deferred or, in some cases, tax-free.

Are you ready? Now go *Make Your Life Tax Deductible*.

Your Form of Organization

This section includes information and strategies pertaining to your form of organization and discusses the advantages and disadvantages of the major forms of business organization that are available to business owners. Also included are specific strategies designed to help you decide which form is best for your business so you can minimize your business income tax liability.

Part 1 includes the following chapters.

Selecting the proper form of business organization for your small business is the first step in the process of making your life tax deductible. As a small-business owner, it's important for you to choose the form of business organization that will provide you with the most advantageous structure and the strongest tax benefits. The good news is that if you don't get it right the first time, you can change your business's form of organization, and you can do so as many times as you wish . . . until you form the proper business structure for your particular small business.

Your goal should be to select the proper form of organization for your business and then maximize the advantages and minimize any disadvantages. The following strategies are applicable only to certain forms of business organization.

STRATEGY 9

Take advantage of the ease of entry afforded business owners by the sole proprietorship form of business organization.

If you want to set up your business entity with a minimum amount of forms and documentation, you are well advised to consider the *sole proprietorship* form of business organization. To start a sole proprietorship, all you have to do is say, "I'm in business." As long as you are engaging in activity in pursuit of profit, the IRS considers you to be "in business." You do not have to file any forms or tax returns until April 15 following the tax year in question. Then and only then are you obliged to tell the IRS about your intentions to operate a business.

Even if you fail to earn a profit the first year, or even for a considerable number of years thereafter, the IRS will continue to assume that you are "trying to make a profit," which is good enough—unless you continue for an inordinate number of years without earning a profit. Then the IRS may consider your activities to be a hobby, and if your activity is considered a hobby, you are not allowed to pass through losses to your individual income tax return, Form 1040, and therefore are not allowed to offset your other income with your business losses. If you do earn a profit, you will owe income taxes at your personal income tax rate.

STRATEGY 10

Pass through business losses from the business to the owner's individual income tax return, Form 1040, to offset the owner's other income.

If you incur business losses, and you have no other business profits against which you could offset these losses, you may be able to offset other personal income appearing on your individual income tax return, Form 1040. On your 1040 Form, you list your income for a given tax year. If you have either a sole proprietorship, a partnership, an S corporation, or a limited liability company (LLC) that you have elected to be taxed as an S corporation, business losses can flow through to your Form 1040 to offset your other income. This means that your other income will be reduced by the dollar amount of these losses, thereby reducing your taxable income and leading to a reduction in your personal income tax liability.

STRATEGY 11

Pass through business profits from the business to the owner's individual income tax return, Form 1040, when the income will be subject to the business owner's lower marginal income tax rate.

If your business entity is either a sole proprietorship, a limited liability company (LLC) taxed as a sole proprietorship, a partnership, an S corporation, or a limited liability company (LLC) that you have elected to be taxed as an S corporation, you are allowed to pass through profits from your business entity directly onto the front page of your individual income tax return (Form 1040).

This is a good idea only if your individual tax rate is lower than the corresponding rate that would apply if your profits were to appear on the separate income tax return of your business entity—such as is the case of either a C corporation or an LLC taxed as a C corporation. The tax rate applicable to the next dollar you earn personally is called your *personal marginal income tax rate*. If this tax rate is less than the corresponding business entity marginal income tax rate, then passing through your business' profits to your individual income tax return (Form 1040) is a positive tax-saving application.

STRATEGY 12

Compensate yourself, as the owner of the business, using distributions of profit.

If the form of your business organization is either a sole proprietorship, a limited liability company (LLC) taxed as a sole proprietorship, a partnership, an S corporation, or an LLC taxed as an S corporation, you are able to take compensation out of your business entity by taking a distribution of profit. In fact, whether or not you actually take any dollars out of your business, you will still be liable for any and all income tax due on the profits of the business. Distributed or undistributed, any tax due is yours to pay. This means that writing a check to yourself, under a distribution-of-profit scenario is a nontaxable event and does not affect your tax liability at all.

STRATEGY 13

**Generate earned income so you may qualify
for certain fringe benefits.**

There are a number of ways to generate earned income for yourself as the owner of a business. One of the major reasons why this is important to you is that unless you generate earned income each tax year, you are not allowed to make contributions to your retirement plan or to qualify for other important fringe benefits. You must have earned income to qualify for contributions to retirement plans.

The ways available to you to generate earned income for yourself vary depending on the form of business organization you select. For example, if your business is a sole proprietorship, a limited liability company (LLC) taxed as a sole proprietorship, or a partnership, a limited liability company (LLC) taxed as a partnership, you can use the bottom-line profit of your business as earned income for you. If you are able to pay yourself wages or guaranteed payments, this form of compensation is also considered earned income.

STRATEGY 14

**Set up your business entity so that it pays your health insurance
premiums and takes a tax deduction for the expense.**

You can deduct 100 percent of health insurance premiums for yourself and your family, up to the extent of your business's net profit (income less expenses). This deduction is available to your business whether you are a sole proprietorship, a limited liability company (LLC) taxed as a sole proprietorship, a partnership, a limited liability company (LLC) taxed as a partnership, an S corporation, or a C corporation.

STRATEGY 15

As the owner, learn how to put dollars in, and take dollars out of, your business.

How you put dollars into your business and, correspondingly, how you take dollars out of your business can have a considerable tax impact on you and/or your business. Therefore, it's important that you move dollars into and out of your business in the proper manner so as not to create additional income tax liability for you and/or your business.

For example, you can always lend dollars to your business entity (except in the case of a sole proprietorship). Then, when you decide to repay the loan to yourself, repayment of the loan does not create any tax liability—the repayment of a loan by your business to yourself is a nontaxable event. The only part of the loan payment that is income to you is any portion of the loan repayment that represents interest.

If you take dollars out of your business in the form of W-2 wages, you are liable for income tax and FICA tax (Social Security and Medicare tax, sometimes called self-employment tax) on any wages or salary paid to you in this manner. Furthermore, your business is liable for the FICA tax matching portion. If your business is either an S corporation or a limited liability company (LLC) taxed as an S corporation, neither you nor your business is liable for the FICA tax.

STRATEGY 16

Select a form of business organization that allows a large enough number of owners.

If your business has more than one owner, you will need to consider a form of business organization other than either a sole proprietorship or a one-member limited liability company (LLC-1). Both of these forms of business organization are restricted to one-owner businesses. If there is more than one owner, you should consider any of the following: a partnership, a multiple-member limited liability company (LLC), an S corporation, or a C corporation. Partnerships, multiple-member limited liability companies (LLCs), and C corporations allow an unlimited number of owners; an S corporation allows up to 75 owners.

STRATEGY 17

Select the form of business organization that offers you protection from unlimited personal liability exposure.

Certain forms of business organization leave their owners exposed to any and all claims against the business. These claims include any debts of the business and/or any successful court judgments against the business. If any of these claims prove to be valid, all the personal assets of all the owners of the business are exposed to be used to pay the debts of, and successful judgments against, the business.

Owners of the following forms of business organization have personal liability exposure: sole proprietorships and partnerships. Limited liability companies and corporations both protect their owners from personal liability exposure. Claims successfully levied against a business that is formed as either a corporation or an LLC stop at the business and do not threaten the personal assets of the owners. The maximum dollar amount any of the owners stand to lose is the cumulative dollar amount each one has invested in their business to date.

STRATEGY 18

Create a business entity that has life beyond your death.

If you want a business entity that survives past your own death, you need to create and use a form of business organization that offers continuity. For example, sole proprietorships and partnerships cease to exist with the death of any owner; the sole proprietorship goes away forever, and the partnership must be reorganized immediately in order to carry on the business functions.

The best way to create a business entity that has continuity past death is to use the corporate form of business organization. The owners of a business that is a corporation are shareholders (owners of stock) in the corporation. When any shareholder dies, the corporate business entity continues on. The outstanding shares owned by the deceased are either bequeathed to the deceased owner's heirs or, in some cases, the outstanding shares are repurchased by the corporation itself. However handled, the business entity goes on and continues to be a viable, functioning, business.

STRATEGY 19

Generate earned income, even if your business doesn't make a profit, by paying yourself either wages or guaranteed payments.

Generating earned income for you as an owner of your business is important for qualifying to make contributions to your retirement plan account. However, if you have been counting on your business generating earned income for you by earning a profit every tax year, and your business suddenly stops making a profit for one or more tax years, your ability to generate earned income for yourself is eliminated unless you take another course of action.

If you are able to pay yourself W-2 wages, even if your business doesn't make a profit, you can generate earned income for yourself by paying yourself either W-2 wages or guaranteed payments, up to the extent of these payments. You will thereby be able to take advantage of any fringe benefits requiring you to have earned income prior to allowing your participation.

STRATEGY 20

Create the opportunity to enjoy the benefits of the "disproportionate splitting of business profits and/or losses" by using the proper form of business organization.

One and only one form of business organization offers the "disproportionate splitting of business profits and/or losses" to its owner, and that's the multiple-member limited liability company (LLC). This allows the disproportionate splitting of member profits and losses (in percentages different from their respective percentages of ownership).

The benefit of using the multiple-member limited liability company (LLC) form of business organization is that the owners are no longer required to tie their share of profits and/or losses to their percentage of ownership in the business. This means that member/owners can enjoy the benefits of receiving profits (and deducting losses) in excess of their individual ownership percentage.

STRATEGY 21

Incorporate, and make the C corporation election if you want to raise large sums of capital.

If you want to raise large sums of money (capital) for your business, the best form of business organization is a C corporation. C corporations are allowed to sell stock to raise capital for business operations. Typically, the stock that is sold is *common stock*, with each share representing a share of ownership in the corporation (i.e., in the business).

Other forms of business organization do not lend themselves to raising considerable capital. The partnership form of business organization has been used as a vehicle to raise money for business operations; however, if large sums of money are required, the corporate form is preferred.

The benefit of the corporate form is that its owners enjoy limited liability, which protects the owners of the business from personal liability exposure should anyone (creditors, successful litigants, etc.) have a legitimate financial claim against the business. In a partnership, the personal assets of all the partners are exposed and can be required to be used to pay any partnership debts and/or judgments.

STRATEGY 22

Choose how your business entity is to be taxed.

To a considerable degree, you, as the owner of your business, can choose how your business will be taxed by your choice of the form of business organization you select in conjunction with tax decisions you can make on behalf of your business.

For example, if you want your business profit and/or loss to flow through to your personal individual income tax return (Form 1040), you should select either a sole proprietorship, a partnership, a limited liability company taxed as either a sole proprietorship, a partnership, or an S corporation, or an S corporation as your form of organization.

If, however, you wish your business to be taxed as a separate entity—apart from your personal income tax return (Form 1040) and your personal income tax rates—you should choose either a limited liability company taxed as a C corporation, or a C corporation. Both of these business entities stand alone, with no impact at all on your personal taxes; they are subject to corporate tax rates only.

STRATEGY 23

Take advantage of the "dividend exclusion" rules and receive business profit that is tax-free to you.

Until recently, any dividends paid to you out of your C corporation were subject to double taxation. The corporation would first have to pay tax on its profits, then it could pay out dividends to its stockholders (you, the owner of the business) out of these after-tax dollars. Then, as the recipient of the dividends, you would have to pay income tax again, this time personally, on the very same dollars. However, with the advent of the relatively new "dividend exclusion" tax laws, you may exclude from double taxation a portion of your business profit that you pay out as dividends.

Now that you are familiar with these overall business form tax strategies, Chapters 1 through 9 examine in depth each form—including its advantages and disadvantages.

CHAPTER 1

Sole Proprietorship

STRATEGY 24

Start out using the sole proprietorship form of business organization.

When you are just getting started as a business owner, you should consider forming a sole proprietorship. You are able to easily and quickly set it up, naming yourself as the sole owner of the business. You are the business. The business is you. All profits (and losses) pass through to your personal tax return.

Advantages

- It's easy to set up. The IRS is notified of your sole proprietorship when you file your tax return on April 15 of the year following the tax year in question. All you have to do to become a sole proprietor is to say you are in business. This means that you are engaging in business activities in pursuit of profit.
- Any losses pass through to the owner's personal income tax return, where they can be used to offset other taxable income.
- Owner is compensated using a distribution of profit. This means the owner can pay him- or herself merely by writing a check whenever personal money is needed (provided the business has the available cash). This eliminates the need to write oneself a payroll check, withhold taxes, pay employment taxes, or file a separate W-2.
  Note: Sole proprietors are still liable for federal, state, and local income taxes, as well as self-employment taxes on the business's bottom-line profit. For this reason, the

owner's tax liability from the business is not a function of how much cash the owner paid him- or herself. You can pay yourself as little or as much as you wish without affecting your tax liability.

- Bottom-line profit is considered "earned income," qualifying the owner for special "fringe benefit" treatment. Since the bottom-line profit is considered earned income to the sole proprietor, he or she can enjoy any fringe benefit that is based on earned income. A prime example of this is your eligibility for a retirement plan. (*Note:* Retirement plans require that you generate a profit and are based on the dollar amount of your earned income.)
- As a sole proprietor, you can deduct 100 percent of health insurance premiums you pay for yourself and your family, up to the extent of your net profit.
- There are benefits to how to put money into and take money out of your business. You and the business are the same entity. Your business dollars are considered to be your personal dollars; therefore, there is no formal way to put dollars into your sole proprietorship except to deposit your personal dollars into the business checking account. This is also true if you obtain a business loan, since a loan to a sole proprietor is considered to be a personal loan that will be used for the business. You, as the owner, take dollars out of the business by paying yourself a distribution of profit. *Note:* You can take dollars out by paying wages to your spouse and/or children and others provided they actually perform work in your business.

Disadvantages

- Multiple ownership is not an option. Only one owner is allowed; if you plan to have more than one owner, you must select an alternative form of organization.
- Profits represent taxable income to the owner, whether or not they are distributed to that owner. Tax information is summarized on a Schedule C, Profit or Loss from Business. The bottom line of Schedule C is considered the profit (or loss) of the sole proprietorship and is included in the owner's individual tax return, Form 1040. This is called a *pass-through* of profit or loss, and therefore sole proprietors are personally liable for tax due on any profit; conversely, they can use a loss to offset other taxable income. As the owner, you are personally liable for tax due on this bottom-line profit, no matter how much you take out in the form of distribution of profit. *Note:* Even if you took nothing out as a distribution of profit, you would still be liable for tax due on the business's bottom-line profit.
- Sole proprietorships are subject to scrutiny under the IRS's so-called hobby rule. If your sole proprietorship shows a profit on your Schedule C, the IRS will "tentatively

presume" that you are "in business" and intending to make a profit. If you show a profit for three of five years, the IRS will apply its "presumptive guideline" that you are in fact in business and attempting to make a profit, not merely engaging in a hobby (which would allow you to deduct expenses only up to the extent of any income). If you fail to show a profit for three of five years, the IRS will *not* automatically disallow your "in business" status, nor will it automatically reject the deductions you took for your business expenses. If required by the IRS, the burden is on you to prove that you are "in business" and intending to make a profit!

- Your profit is subject to self-employment tax. The bottom-line profit is considered earned income and is subject to self-employment tax equal to 12.4 percent of profit shown, up to $90,000 for Social Security, plus 2.9 percent of all profit for Medicare. *Note:* You can deduct half of the self-employment tax you pay on your individual tax return (Form 1040).
- You are subject to unlimited personal liability. As a sole proprietor, you are personally liable for any debts, judgments, or other successful legal claims against your business.
- There is no continuity after death. When the owner dies, the sole proprietorship ceases to exist.

Although the sole proprietorship form of business organization is often the best form to begin with, several intrinsic characteristics of a sole proprietorship make it less than desirable, and in some instances totally inappropriate, for your business.

The sole proprietorship form of organization allows only one (sole) owner; if there's more than one owner, this form isn't an option. Also, any and all profits of the sole proprietorship are considered earned income and therefore are subject to an additional tax of 15.3 percent (for Social Security and Medicare). Furthermore, the owner of a sole proprietorship is personally liable for the financial obligations of the business. This means that all the owner's personal assets are at risk for business debts and court judgments.

CHAPTER 2

Partnership

STRATEGY 25

Start out using the partnership form of business organization if you start up with one or more partners.

If your business has more than one owner (that is, if you have one or more partners in your business), you may want to consider the partnership form of organization. This form accommodates more than one owner and allows you to split the profits (and any losses) between you and the other owners (partners) in proportion to each partner's percentage share of ownership (i.e., his or her profit/loss sharing percentage).

Advantages

- Multiple ownership is an option. There can be an unlimited number of owners (called *partners*) in a partnership.
- Partners are considered "active owners." Therefore the bottom-line profit is considered "earned income," qualifying the partners for special "fringe benefit" treatment: The bottom-line profit of the partnership is reported to each partner on a pro rata basis using Schedule K-1 and is considered earned income to the partner(s). This means that any profit can be used to qualify a partner for fringe benefits that are based on a partner having earned income.
- Partners can take distributions of profit without affecting their tax liability. Partners can be paid their pro rata share of profits without the dollar amount of these distribu-

tions having any impact on their income tax liability. *Note:* Partners are liable for any tax due on the profit of the partnership, whether or not they take—and without regard to the dollar amount of—any distributions.

- This form can compensate partners using "guaranteed payments" (for services rendered), which are considered "earned income" to the recipient. The dollar amount of these guaranteed payments is considered earned income, thus allowing the partners fringe benefits (whether or not the partnership earns a profit) that require earned income to qualify for a retirement plan.
- Any losses pass through to an owner's personal income tax return, where they can be used to offset other income. Since each partner is liable for his or her pro rata share of profits, each can also use this pro rata share of any losses to offset other taxable income on his or her own individual (Form 1040) tax return.
- As a partner, you can deduct 100 percent of health insurance premiums you pay for yourself and your family, up to the extent of your net profit.
- Partners may put money into and take money out of the business. Each partner can contribute capital or other assets to the partnership, or lend the partnership money to add dollars or value to the partnership. Partners can withdraw dollars by taking a repayment of a loan (plus interest), by a distribution of profits, or by a guaranteed payment.

Disadvantages

- Owners' pro rata share of profits represent taxable income to partners, whether or not they are distributed to the partners. Tax information goes on an information-only partnership return, Form 1065. The bottom line of Form 1065 is considered the total profit (or loss) of the partnership. A Schedule K-1 is prepared for each partner, reflecting his or her individual share of the partnership's total profit (or loss). This information on Schedule K-1 is then transferred to the individual owner's tax return, Form 1040. Each partner is personally responsible for tax due based on the bottom-line profit on their individual Schedule K-1s.
- The profit is subject to self-employment tax. The bottom-line profit of a partnership is considered earned income and is therefore subject to self-employment tax equal to 12.4 percent of profit shown, up to $90,000 for Social Security, plus 2.9 percent of all profit for Medicare. *Note:* You can deduct half of the self-employment tax you pay on your individual tax return (Form 1040).
- As a partner, you are not allowed to pay yourself wages. You can, however, be compensated using "guaranteed payments." All guaranteed payments are considered earned income and are subject to self-employment tax.

- You are subject to unlimited personal liability. As a general partner, you are liable for all partnership debts, successful lawsuits resulting in a judgment, and any other liability the partnership incurs.
- There is no continuity after death. When any of the partners die, the partnership ceases to exist and must then be re-formed.

Although the partnership form of organization allows for multiple owners, each one being a partner in the business, each partner is still personally liable for the financial obligations of the business. This means that the personal assets of all the partners are exposed to any and all creditors' claims and court judgments against the partnership. Any and all profits of the partnership are considered earned income and are therefore subject to an additional tax of 15.3 percent (for Social Security and Medicare).

CHAPTER 3

Limited Partnership

STRATEGY 26

Select the limited partnership form of business organization if you start up with one or more business partners and you wish to insulate your assets from personal liability exposure, right from the start.

If your business has more than one owner (i.e., you have one or more partners in your business) and you want to insulate the partners from personal liability exposure, you may want to consider a limited partnership form of business organization. This form accommodates more than one owner and allows you to split the profits (and any losses) between all the owners (partners) in proportion to each partner's percentage share of ownership (i.e., his or her profit/loss sharing percentage). The additional benefit of a limited partnership (over a partnership) is the protection from personal liability exposure that a limited partnership provides for the partnership's "limited partners." This means that the maximum dollar amount that each limited partner can lose is the amount of dollars that each one has invested in the partnership. Each limited partnership has a general partner, who is responsible for managing the partnership's business activities, and any number of limited partners, who are not considered active participants in the business operations. The general partner does not enjoy this protection from personal liability exposure. Furthermore, the limited partners (only) also enjoy having their share of the profits being exempt from the 15.3 percent Social Security plus Medicare tax. (General partners must pay this 15.3 percent tax on their share of profits.)

Advantages

- Multiple ownership is an option. There can be an unlimited number of owners (called *partners*) in a partnership.
- The general partner's share of bottom-line profit is considered "earned income" (because the general partner is considered to be an active owner), therefore qualifying the general partner for special "fringe benefit" treatment: The bottom-line profit of the partnership, which is reported to each partner on a pro rata basis using a Schedule K-1, is considered earned income to the general partner. This means that any profit can be used to qualify the general partner for fringe benefits that are based on a partner having earned income.
- The limited partners' share of the bottom-line profit of the limited partnership is not considered earned income and is therefore not subject to self-employment tax.
- Partners can take distributions of profit without affecting their tax liability. Partners can be paid their pro rata share of profits without the dollar amount of these distributions having any impact on their income tax liability. *Note:* Partners are liable for any tax due on the profit of the partnership, whether they take or not, and without regard to the dollar amount of any distributions.
- Owners can be compensated using "guaranteed payments," which are considered "earned income" to the recipient. The dollar amount of these guaranteed payments is considered earned income, thus allowing the partners fringe benefits that require earned income to qualify (e.g., a retirement plan).
- Limited partner losses are considered passive losses, and they pass through to the limited partners' personal income tax returns, where they can be used to offset other passive income. Since each limited partner is liable for his or her pro rata share of profits, each can also use this pro rata share of any losses (considered passive) to offset other passive income on his or her own individual (Form 1040) tax return. *Exception:* If a limited partner's participation in the business is determined (by the IRS) to be material (one definition of *material participation* is greater than 500 hours per year) *or* if the limited partner receives guaranteed payments from the partnership (for services rendered), then the limited partner's share of partnership income is considered earned income.
- The general partner of a limited partnership can deduct 100 percent of the health insurance premiums he or she pays for personal and family protection . . . up to the extent of his or her pro rata share of the limited partnership's net profit (because the profit is considered earned income). *Note:* If a limited partner has earned income, he or she will also qualify.

- There is limited personal liability for limited partners (from outsiders, from the limited partnership itself, and from other partners). *Note:* The general partner is subject to unlimited personal liability.
- Partners may put money into and take money out of the business. Each partner can contribute capital or other assets to the partnership, or lend the partnership money to add dollars or value to the partnership. A partner can withdraw dollars by taking a repayment of a loan (plus interest), by a distribution of profits, or by a guaranteed payment.

Disadvantages

- The general partner's share of the bottom-line profit of the limited partnership is considered earned income and is subject to self-employment tax equal to 12.4 percent of profit shown, up to $90,000 for Social Security, plus 2.9 percent of all profit for Medicare. *Note:* You can deduct half of the self-employment tax you pay on your individual tax return (Form 1040).
- The limited partners' share of bottom-line profit is not considered "earned income," because the limited partner is considered to be an inactive owner. Therefore, the limited partners do not qualify for special "fringe benefit" treatment. The bottom-line profit of the partnership, which is reported to each limited partner on a pro rata basis using a Schedule K-1, is not considered earned income to the limited partners. This means that any profit cannot be used to qualify the limited partners for fringe benefits that are based on a limited partner having earned income. *Exception:* If a limited partner's participation in the business is determined (by the IRS) to be material (one definition of *material participation* is greater than 500 hours per year) *or* if the limited partner receives guaranteed payments from the partnership (for services rendered), then the limited partner's share of partnership income is considered earned income.
- Owners' pro rata share of profits represents taxable income to partners, whether or not they are distributed to the partners. Tax information goes on an information-only partnership return, Form 1065. The bottom line of Form 1065 is considered the total profit (or loss) of the partnership. A Schedule K-1 is prepared for each partner, reflecting his or her individual share of the partnership's total profit (or loss). This information on the Schedule K-1 is then transferred to the individual owner's tax return, Form 1040. Each partner is personally responsible for tax due based on the bottom-line profit on their individual Schedule K-1s.

- The general partner is not allowed to pay him- or herself wages, but can be compensated using guaranteed payments. All guaranteed payments are considered earned income and are subject to self-employment tax.
- The general partner is liable for all partnership debts, successful lawsuits resulting in a judgment, or any other liability the partnership incurs.
- There is no continuity after death. When a partner dies, the partnership ceases to exist and must be re-formed.

Although a limited partnership does allow for multiple owners and does protect its limited partners from personal liability exposure, the limited partnership's general partner does not have such personal liability protection. And, although the limited partners do enjoy the fact that their pro rata share of profit is exempt from the 15.3 percent Social Security plus Medicare tax, the general partner's profit is subject to this 15.3 percent tax.

CHAPTER 4

One-Member Limited Liability Company (LLC-1)

STRATEGY 27

Select the one-member limited liability company (LLC-1) form of business organization as soon as possible—certainly before your small business begins operations.

If you are the only owner of your business, the one-member limited liability company offers some advantages. First of all, an LLC can be easily and quickly set up through your state's "department of state"—often online. And unless you indicate otherwise, your one-member LLC will be taxed as a sole proprietorship—with all profits (and losses) passing through to your personal income tax return. However, the LLC form of business organization offers an additional advantage—the opportunity for you to elect to have your LLC taxed as either an S or a C corporation if you wish. This election option allows you to create considerable tax savings from the tax rates applicable to the corporate tax structure. If you want the profits to flow through to your personal tax return (and be taxed at your personal tax rate) and to be exempt from the 15.3 percent Social Security plus Medicare tax, you should elect for your LLC to be taxed as an S corporation. If you wish to have the profits taxed at the corporate tax rate (which may be lower than your personal tax rate) and also to have the profits exempt from the 51.3 percent Social Security plus Medicare tax, you should elect for your LLC to be taxed as a C corporation. The C corporation offers the additional advantage of paying (out of the C corporation's after-tax profit) tax-free dividends to yourself (under dividend exclusion tax law). Perhaps the best advantage of an LLC is that it provides personal liability protection to you, the owner.

Advantages

- There is limited personal liability for the owner (called a *member*). The member, who in this instance is also the "managing member," enjoys limited liability, which means that the member is personally protected from any liability of the LLC, from successful judgments, and from the LLC itself.
- Any losses pass through to the owner's personal income tax return, where they can be used to offset other taxable income.
- As owner, you are compensated using a distribution of profit. This means you can pay yourself merely by writing a check—whenever you need the money (provided the business has the available cash). This eliminates the need to write oneself a payroll check, withhold taxes, pay employment taxes, or file a W-2 throughout the year. *Note:* The member is still liable for federal, state, and local income taxes, as well as self-employment taxes on the business's bottom-line profit. For this reason, your tax liability from the business is not a function of how much cash you, as the owner, pay yourself. You can pay yourself as little or as much as you wish without affecting your tax liability.
- Bottom-line profit is considered "earned income," qualifying the owner for special "fringe benefit" treatment. Since this bottom-line profit is considered earned income to the one-person LLC (who is required to file a Schedule C for the business, just like a sole proprietor), you can enjoy any fringe benefit that is based on earned income. A prime example of this is your eligibility for a retirement plan (*Note:* Retirement plans require, and are based on the dollar amount of, earned income).
- As a member of a one-person LLC, you can deduct 100 percent of health insurance premiums you pay for yourself and your family, up to the extent of your net profit.
- Your business's dollars are considered to be your personal dollars; therefore, there is no formal way to put dollars into your LLC except to merely deposit your personal dollars into the business checking account. This is also true if you obtain a business loan, since a loan to an LLC member is considered to be a personal loan that will be used for the business.

    As the owner, you can take dollars out of the business by paying yourself a distribution of profit. *Note:* You can take dollars out (as a family unit) by paying wages to your spouse, provided he or she works in your business.
- The member of a one-member LLC can elect for their LLC to be taxed as a corporation (S or C) instead of as a sole proprietorship. This requires filing IRS Form 8832. Remember, if you elect to be taxed as either an S or a C corporation, you must follow the rules of corporate tax law.

Disadvantages

- Profits represent taxable income to the owner—whether or not they are distributed to the owner. Tax information is summarized on a Schedule C, Profit or Loss from Business. The bottom line of Schedule C is considered the profit (or loss) of the LLC and is included in the owner's individual tax return, Form 1040. This is called a *pass-through* of profit or loss, and the member is personally liable for tax due on any profit (or can use a loss to offset other taxable income). You, as the owner, are personally liable for tax due on this bottom line-profit, no matter how much you take out in the form of distribution of profit. *Note:* Even if you took nothing out as a distribution of profit, you would still be liable for tax due on the business's bottom-line profit.

- Businesses using this form are subject to an additional level of scrutiny under the IRS's hobby rule. If your one-member LLC shows a profit on your Schedule C, the IRS will "tentatively presume" that you are "in business" and intending to make a profit. If you show a profit for three years running, the IRS will apply its "presumptive guideline" that you are in fact "in business" and attempting to make a profit, not merely engaging in a hobby (which would allow you to deduct expenses only up to the extent of any income). If you fail to show a profit for three years in a row, the IRS will *not* automatically disallow your "in business" status, nor will it automatically reject the deductions you took for your business expenses. The IRS will, however, reserve the right to audit you, and the burden is on you to prove that you are "in business" and intending to make a profit!

- Since the bottom-line profit of a one-member LLC is considered earned income, this profit is subject to self-employment tax equal to 12.4 percent of profit shown, up to $90,000 for Social Security, plus 2.9 percent of all profit for Medicare. *Note:* You can deduct half of the self-employment tax you pay on your individual tax return (Form 1040).

- There is no continuity after death. When you, as the owner, die, the one-member LLC ceases to exist.

If you are not the only owner of your business, a one-member LLC is not applicable. However, fortunately, you have the multiple-member LLC available to you, which provides for more than one owner (member).

Multiple-Member Limited Liability Company (LLC)

STRATEGY 28

Select the multiple-member limited liability company (LLC) form of business organization as soon as possible if you start up with one or more business partners, and certainly before your small business begins operations.

If you are not the only owner of your business, the multiple-member limited liability company offers some advantages. First of all, an LLC can be easily and quickly set up through your state's "department of state"—often online. And unless you indicate otherwise, your multiple-member LLC will be taxed as a partnership—with each member's pro rate share of profits (and losses) passing through to his or her personal income tax return. However, the LLC form of business organization offers an additional advantage—the opportunity for you to elect to have your LLC taxed as either an S or a C corporation if you wish. This election option allows you to create considerable tax savings from the tax rates applicable to the corporate tax structure. If you want each member's pro rata share of profits to flow through to the member's personal tax return (and be taxed at his or her personal tax rate) and to be exempt from the 15.3 percent Social Security plus Medicare tax, you should elect for your LLC to be taxed as an S corporation. If you wish to have the profits taxed at the corporate tax rate (which may be lower than the member's personal tax rates) and also to have the profits exempt from the 51.3 percent Social Security plus Medicare tax, you should elect for your LLC to be taxed as a C corporation. The C corporation offers the additional advantage of paying (out of the C corporation's after-tax profit) tax-free dividends to the members (under dividend exclusion tax law). Additionally, each member's prorated share (percent) of profit (or loss) can be different than his or her ownership share (percent). This means each member's share of profits (and losses) can be disproportionate to (different from) his or her ownership share. Perhaps the best advantage of an LLC is that it provides personal liability protection to all its member/owners.

Advantages

- Multiple ownership is an option. An LLC allows an unlimited number of owners (called *members*).
- This setup allows for the special allocation of profits, or the disproportionate splitting of member profits and losses (in percentages different from their respective percentages of ownership). This means that members can enjoy the benefits of receiving profits (and deducting losses) in excess of their individual ownership percentage.
- Members enjoy limited liability, which means that they are personally protected from any liability of the LLC, from successful judgments, and from the LLC itself.
- The managing member's share of bottom-line profit is considered "earned income" (because the managing member is considered to be an active owner), thereby qualifying the managing member for special "fringe benefit" treatment. The bottom-line profit of the LLC, which is reported to each member on a pro rata basis using a Schedule K-1, is considered earned income to the managing member. This means that any profit can be used to qualify the managing member for fringe benefits that are based on a member having earned income.
- Members' shares of the bottom-line profit of an LLC are not considered earned income and therefore not subject to self-employment tax.
- Members are compensated using either distributions of profit or guaranteed payments. A distribution of profit allows each member to pay him- or herself merely by writing checks, whenever he or she needs the money (provided the business has the available cash). This eliminates the need to write oneself payroll checks, withhold taxes, pay employment taxes, or file a W-2. *Note:* Members are still liable for federal, state, and local income taxes on their pro rata share of the business's bottom-line profit. For this reason, the members' tax liability from the business is not a function of how much cash they paid themselves. They can pay themselves as little or as much as they wish without affecting the other members' liability. The other way members can be compensated is by receiving guaranteed payments, which represent earned

income to members, thereby qualifying them to enjoy the advantages of tax-favored fringe benefits that are based on the amount of each member's earned income. An example of this type of fringe benefit is a retirement plan.

- The managing member of an LLC can deduct 100 percent of the health insurance premiums he or she pays for personal and family coverage, up to the extent of his or her pro rata share of the LLC's net profit (because the profit is considered earned income). *Note:* If members have earned income, they will also qualify.
- A corporation can be a "member" (an owner) of an LLC. This allows the creation of an additional level of ownership. This is designed to create an entity that can offer such traditional fringe benefits as retirement plans, as well as an additional level of protection from liability.
- Each member can contribute capital or other assets to the LLC or lend money to the LLC to add dollars or value to the business. Members can withdraw dollars by taking a repayment of a loan (plus interest), a distribution of profit, or a guaranteed payment.
- There is continuity after death. If a member dies, the LLC can continue to exist, subject to the unanimous positive vote of all remaining members, thus allowing the LLC to remain in business.
- Members of an LLC can elect for their LLC to be taxed as a corporation (C or S) instead of as a partnership. This requires filing IRS Form 8832.

Disadvantages

- Each member's pro rata share of profits represents taxable income, whether or not their share of profits is distributed to the member. Tax information is summarized on a Form 1065, U.S. Partnership Return of Income. The bottom line of Form 1065 is considered the profit (or loss) of the LLC. A pro rata share of total profit (each member's share) is included in the owner's individual tax return, Form 1040. This is called a *pass-through* of profit or loss, and the member is personally liable for tax due on any profit (or can use a loss to offset other taxable income). As an owner, you are personally liable for tax due on this bottom-line profit, no matter how much you take out in the form of distribution of profit. *Note:* Even if you took nothing out as a distribution of profit, you would still be liable for tax due on the business's bottom-line profit.
- The managing member's share of the bottom-line profit of the LLC is considered earned income and is subject to self-employment tax equal to 12.4 percent of profit shown, up to $90,000 for Social Security, plus 2.9 percent of all profit for Medicare. *Note:* You can deduct half of the self-employment tax you pay on your individual tax return (Form 1040).

- The members' share of bottom-line profit is not considered "earned income" (because the members are considered to be inactive owners); therefore, the members do not qualify for special tax-favored "fringe benefit" treatment. The bottom-line profit of the LLC, which is reported to each member on a pro rata basis using a Schedule K-1, is not considered earned income to the member. This means that any profit cannot be used to qualify the members for fringe benefits that are based on a member having earned income. *Exception:* If a member's participation in the business is determined (by the IRS) to be *material* (one definition of material participation is greater than 500 hours per year) *or* if the member receives guaranteed payments from the LLC (for services rendered), then the members' share of partnership income is considered earned income.

One of the biggest disadvantages of the multiple-member LLC is the fact that the managing member's share of the bottom-line profit of the LLC is considered earned income and thus subject to the 15.3 percent Social Security plus Medicare tax. Although the nonmanaging member's pro rata share of profits is exempt from this 15.3 percent tax, the managing member's share is not.

CHAPTER 6

S Corporation

STRATEGY 29

**Select the S corporation form of business organization if
your personal income tax rate is less than the tax rate applicable
to your business.**

Many of the advantages of the S corporation form of business organization are similar to those of the multiple-member LLC. If you are not the only owner of your business, the S corporation offers some advantages. First of all, an S corporation can be easily and quickly set up through your state's "department of state"—often online. Unless you indicate otherwise, your S corporation will be taxed as a C corporation. Under an S corporation, each shareholder's (i.e., owner's) pro rata share of profits flow through to the shareholder's personal tax return (and are taxed at that personal tax rate) and are exempt from the 15.3 percent Social Security plus Medicare tax. Just as with an LLC, an S corporation provides personal liability protection to all its shareholder/owners.

Advantages

- Both single- and multiple-ownership (called shareholders) options are available. An S corporation can be owned by either a single shareholder (owner) or multiple shareholders (up to a maximum of 75 shareholders).
- Personal liability is limited. The shareholder(s) of an S corporation enjoy protection from personal liability; they are liable only up to the extent of their contribution plus retained capital in the corporation.

- Profit is *not* subject to self-employment tax. The bottom-line profit of an S corporation is not considered earned income, and therefore it is not subject to self-employment tax.
- Owners may be compensated via wages, which are considered "earned income" to the recipient: As a shareholder of an S corporation, if you work in the business, you are allowed to pay yourself a fair and reasonable wage for work you perform. If you do not work in an S corporation, you are not required to pay yourself wages. When you pay yourself a wage or salary (W-2 wages), it is considered earned income to you. This earned income can qualify you for certain fringe benefits, such as your participation in a retirement plan, that are based on earned income.
- Any losses that pass through to an owner's personal income tax return can be used to offset other income. In other words, your pro rata share (based on your percentage of ownership) of any losses generated by the S corporation will be shown on a Schedule K-1 when you are preparing your personal individual income tax return (Form 1040). These losses can be used to offset other income shown on your Form 1040.
- Owners can be compensated using a distribution of profit. Whenever you, as a shareholder of an S corporation, wish, you can simply write yourself a check drawn on corporate funds (provided that funds are available to do so). This payment to you is part of your pro rata share of the S corporation's distribution of profit.
- As a shareholder in an S corporation, you can put dollars into the business by either lending dollars to the corporation or by investing your dollars in the corporation in the form of contributed capital. Conversely, you can take dollars out of the corporation by either receiving repayments of the loan tax-free (plus taxable interest), by paying yourself wages or a salary, or by taking distributions of profit out of the corporation.
- Medical insurance for an officer/shareholder is deductible to the extent of wages.
- There is continuity after death of owner(s). If one shareholder dies, the S corporation continues to exist. This means you do not have to re-form an S corporation when a co-owner dies.

Disadvantages

- Bottom-line profit is *not* considered "earned income," thus disqualifying owners from special "fringe benefit" treatment.
- Shareholders' pro rata share of profits represents taxable income to recipients, whether or not they are distributed to each shareholder. An S corporation is not considered a

"tax entity," but rather, each owner receives a Schedule K-1 showing his or her pro rata share of profit. Form 1120-S (information-only) is filed showing total profit; the individual S corporation owners annually receive Schedule K-1 detailing their allocated shares of the S corporation's profit for the year. Each owner is responsible for paying tax on the dollar amount of his or her shares of the S corporation's profit. Owners do this by including this profit on the front side of their individual tax return, Form 1040.

- An S corporation cannot be owned by another corporation or by a partnership. This limits the use of an S corporation form of organization in combination with another entity.
- An S corporation is limited to a maximum of 75 owners (called *shareholders*), all of whom must be U.S. residents or citizens.
- Shareholders/owners of an S corporation must take some (reasonable) wages. This does have the benefit of creating earned income to the shareholders, thereby qualifying them for tax-deductible fringe benefits such as medical insurance.
- Distributions of profit to shareholders/owners must be *proportionate* (i.e., must be made in the very same proportion as their ownership percentage).

The Subchapter S corporation form of organization allows for multiple owners, called *shareholders*, only up to a maximum of 75 shareholders. If you want or need more shareholders, the S corporation is not applicable for your business. Also, you may not wish to have the profits flow through to your personal tax return—your personal tax rates may be higher than the corresponding C corporation tax rates. In addition, under a C corporation, shareholder medical expenses are not deductible as a corporate expense.

CHAPTER 7

C Corporation

STRATEGY 30

Select the C corporation form of business organization if you wish to raise capital by selling shares of stock and/or reinvest the business profits back into the business and/or take profits out of the business (tax-free to you personally).

Many of the advantages of the C corporation form of business organization are similar to those of the S corporation. If you are not the only owner of your business, the C corporation offers some advantages. For example, the C corporation form of organization allows for an unlimited number of owners, called *shareholders*. A C corporation can be easily and quickly set up through your state's "department of state"—often online. Unless you indicate otherwise, your corporation will be taxed as a C corporation.

By being a C corporation, you also have the opportunity to create considerable tax savings from the tax rates applicable to the corporate tax structure (which may be lower than the shareholder's personal tax rates), and all the C corporation's bottom-line profit is exempt from the 15.3 percent Social Security plus Medicare tax. A C corporation offers the additional advantage of paying the members dividends (out of the C corporation's after-tax profit) that are tax-free to the members (under dividend exclusion tax law). A C corporation provides personal liability protection to all its shareholder/owners. Finally, if you wish to raise capital (money) for your business, you can do so by selling shares of stock in your C corporation to investors outside of your business who do not take part in the operation of your business.

Advantages

- Both single- and multiple-ownership (called shareholders) options are available. A C corporation can be owned by a single shareholder or by an unlimited number of shareholder (i.e., owners).
- Personal liability is limited. The shareholder(s) of a C corporation enjoy protection from personal liability; they are liable only up to the extent of their contribution plus retained capital in the corporation.
- Profit is *not* subject to self-employment tax. The bottom-line profit of a C corporation is not considered earned income, and therefore it is not subject to self-employment tax.
- Owners may be compensated via wages, which are considered "earned income to the recipient." As owner of a C corporation, if you work in the business, you are allowed to pay yourself a fair and reasonable wage for work you perform. When you pay yourself a wage or salary (W-2 wages), it is considered earned income to you. This earned income can qualify you for fringe benefits, such as your participation in a retirement plan, based on earned income. The only other way you can receive compensation as an owner is through dividend payouts. A word of caution: Dividends are subject to double taxation—once at the corporate level, because dividends are paid out of after-tax dollars, and again to the individual owner, as investment income—unless they qualify under "dividend exclusion."
- Profit is subject to corporate income tax rates. A C corporation is its own tax entity and files Form 1120, U.S. Corporation Income Tax Return. The bottom-line profit shown on this return is subject to corporate income tax, starting at 15 percent (which may be lower than the personal income tax rate(s) of the owner(s).
- A shareholder in a C corporation can put dollars into the business by either lending dollars to the corporation or by investing dollars in the corporation, whereby the shareholder receives stock in the corporation in exchange for contributed capital. Conversely, the shareholder can take dollars out of the corporation by either receiving repayments of the loan (tax-free plus taxable interest), by paying him- or herself wages or a salary, or by receiving corporate dividends.
- The owner of a C corporation can elect to be treated (for tax purposes) as an S corporation. This requires filing IRS Form 2553. *Note:* This option can now be elected retroactively—not just within the first three months of any fiscal year (as was previously the tax law). If you can show reasonable cause for the late filing, this election can be made within 12 months of the original due date of the election, but in no case later than the unextended due date of the tax return for the year in which the C corporation intends to be taxed as an S corporation.

43

- The medical expenses of shareholders/owners in a C corporation are deduct under a (formally established and maintained) medical reimbursement plan.
- There is continuity after death of owner(s). If one shareholder dies, the C corpc tion continues to exist. This means you do not have to re-form a C corporation w a co-owner dies.
- You are subject to the dividend exclusion. When a C corporation pays dividends to its shareholders, these dividends are paid out of after-tax profits (after corporate profits have been paid). However, under the dividend exclusion tax laws, a portion of the C corporation's after-tax profits can be distributed to shareholders in the form of dividends, which are tax-free to the shareholder recipients. This share of C corporation profits is called the *excludable dividend amount*. The formula for determining the EDA, in example form, is given in Table 7.1. Under the the scenario in Table 7.1, this C corporation could pay a tax-free dividend to its shareholders.

Disadvantages

- Owners are limited to two ways of taking compensation out of the corporation: Shareholders of a C corporation can either pay themselves W-2 wages, which are subject to both self-employment tax and income tax (at the owner's personal income tax rate), or they can pay themselves dividends, which are subject to double taxation (taxed at both the corporate and individual income tax level, unless they qualify under "dividend exclusion").

Table 7.1 Computing Excludable Dividend Amount (EDA)

Dollar amount of the C corporation's taxable income	$100,000
Using a 34% corporate income tax rate	× .34
Dollar amount of U.S. tax due	$ 34,000
Dollar amount of the C corporation's taxable income	$100,000
Dollar amount of U.S. tax due	($ 34,000)
Excludable dividend amount (EDA)	$ 66,000

here's no pass-through of any losses to owner's personal income tax return. Corporate losses do not pass through to the shareholder's personal tax returns and therefore do not potentially offset any of the shareholders other taxable income.

- If you are set up as a C corporation providing personal services (e.g., health, law, engineering, architecture, accounting, actuarial sciences, performing arts, or consulting) and you own more than 50 percent of the stock in your C corporation, you may be classified as a "personal services corporation" and subject to a flat 35 percent tax rate on all your corporate profit.

The biggest disadvantage to being a C corporation is the potential for it to be treated as a personal services corporation subject to a flat 35 percent tax rate on all corporate profit. The best way to avoid being treated as a personal services corporation is to elect to be an S corporation, since an S corporation is by definition not treated as a personal services corporation. Another disadvantage is that, unless the corporation's profits qualify for the dividend exclusion (making dividends paid out of the corporation's after-tax profits tax-free to the shareholders that receive corporate dividends), shareholders are limited in how they can be compensated; other than dividends, shareholders can be compensated by receiving W-2 wages (which are subject to both the 15.3 percent Social Security plus Medicare tax *and* the shareholder's highest (marginal) personal income tax rate.

CHAPTER 8

Limited Partnership Plus C Corporation

STRATEGY 31

Select a combination of a limited partnership plus a C corporation form of business organization if you want to convert your limited partnership to a single-owner situation.

The limited partnership form of organization allows for multiple owners: Each is a partner who enjoys limited liability, except the general partner (in this instance the C corporation), which is liable for the financial obligations of the partnership. The partners in the limited partnership are also the shareholders of the C corporation. The profits or losses of the limited partnership pass directly through to the owner's personal income tax return, Form 1040. The limited partnership files a Form 1065 and lists each partner's taxable profit on a Schedule K-1. *Note:* The C corporation also receives a Schedule K-1. The bottom-line profit of the limited partnership is not considered to be earned income to the partners and therefore is *not* subject to self-employment tax.

The combination of a limited partnership and a C corporation creates a situation whereby the C corporation becomes the general partner (owner) in the limited partnership. You are both a limited partner (owner) in the partnership and a shareholder (owner) in the C corporation.

Advantages

- The limited partnership can, by adding a C corporation, accommodate a single-owner situation. The limited partnership will have more than one partner (owner), as is required, consisting of you as an individual plus the C corporation in which you are the sole owner. Thus you own 100 percent of the corporation's stock, but as two entities.

- The limited partnership can have as partners (owners) both an individual and the C corporation (simultaneously). This allows you to structure, as one of your partners, an entity (the C corporation) that can accumulate cash at a beginning tax rate of 15 percent (which can be lower than yours) and that can serve as a framework offering fringe benefits to you, such as a retirement plan.
- The C corporation can be the general partner of the limited partnership. You can be the sole owner of the C corporation, and in that role you can make decisions for your limited partnership without having to personally assume the liability associated with being the general partner of your limited partnership.
- The individual can be a limited partner in the limited partnership. As a limited partner, you enjoy protection from partnership liability while enjoying the benefits of being able to profit directly from the activities of the partnership.
- The limited partnership can compensate its partners, including your C corporation, using "distributions of profit." You and your C corporation are both limited partners in the partnership, and as such can both receive distributions of profits from the partnership.
- There exists limited personal liability for the owners of both the limited partnership and the C corporation. As the owner of a limited partnership and a C corporation, you enjoy the benefits of no exposure to the current or future liabilities of either entity.
- The limited partnership can compensate the individual owner using "guaranteed payments," which are considered "earned income" to the recipient. You can receive guaranteed payments from the partnership, and this creates earned income for you, by which you qualify for fringe benefits (e.g., retirement plan participation).
- The limited partnership can compensate the C corporation using "consulting or management fees," which are considered income to the C corporation. Cash can be moved out of the partnership into the C corporation. This cash can then be used to fund the activities of your C corporation.
- The C corporation can compensate owners using wages, which are considered "earned income" to the recipient(s). You can take cash out of your C corporation in the form of earned income by having your corporation pay you wages.
- The bottom-line profit of limited partnership is *not* considered earned income and is therefore exempt from self-employment tax, although each partner's pro rata share of partnership profit does represent taxable income to the partners.

- Any losses of the limited partnership pass through to its owners' tax returns, whereby these losses can be used to offset other taxable income. Should the partnership generate a loss (hopefully just a "paper loss" created by implementing tax strategies), partners can use their own pro rata share of any losses to offset other taxable income on their personal income tax returns.

- Profits of the limited partnership can be upstreamed to the corporation, where these profits may enjoy lower tax rates. This can be accomplished by the payment of a "consulting or management fee" from the limited partnership to the C corporation and by the limited partnership making a "distribution of its profits" to the C corporation.

- Upstreamed profits can (1) be sheltered by tax-deductible business expenses of the C corporation and (2) provide "earned income," allowing the C corporation to use this earned income as the basis for qualified retirement plan(s) for its (wage-earning) employees.

- The limited partnership partners' (i.e., owners') pro rata share of profits represent taxable income to the C corporation's general partner, whether or not they are distributed. This means this profit is upstreamed, whether or not it is distributed (in full or in part). Profits can be upstreamed to the C corporation, whether or not they are actually distributed (e.g., in cash). The corporation's pro rata share of the partnership's bottom-line profit is automatically upstreamed to the corporation for tax purposes.

- The C corporation can compensate its shareholders using wages, which are considered "earned income to the recipient." As the shareholder (i.e., owner) of a C corporation, if you work in the business you are allowed to pay yourself a fair and reasonable wage for work you perform. This wage or salary (W-2 wages) is considered earned income to you. This earned income allows you to qualify for fringe benefits, such as your participation in a retirement plan, based on earned income.

- You are subject to the dividend exclusion. When a C corporation pays dividends to its shareholders, these dividends are paid out of after-tax profits (after corporate profits have been paid). However, under the dividend exclusion tax laws, a portion of the C corporation's after-tax profits can be distributed to shareholders in the form of dividends, which are tax-free to the shareholder recipients. This share of C corporation profits is called the *excludable dividend amount*. The formula for determining the EDA, in example form, is shown in Table 8.1. Under the scenario in Table 8.1, this C corporation could pay a tax-free dividend to its shareholders.

Table 8.1   Computing Excludable Dividend Amount (EDA)

Dollar amount of the 　　C corporation's taxable income	$100,000
Using a 34% corporate income tax rate	× .34
Dollar amount of U.S. tax due	$ 34,000
Dollar amount of the 　　C corporation's taxable income	$100,000
Dollar amount of U.S. tax due	($ 34,000)
Excludable dividend amount (EDA)	$ 66,000

Disadvantages

- The owners' pro rata share of profits represents taxable income to the general partner (the C corporation) and to any limited partners, whether or not the profits are distributed. This means that partners can have tax liability for profits they did receive, as well as tax liability for profits they never received (the portion of the limited partnership profits that were not distributed).
- Owners are limited to two ways of taking compensation out of the corporation: Shareholders of a C corporation can either pay themselves W-2 wages, which are subject to both self-employment tax and income tax (at the owner's personal income tax rate), or they can pay themselves dividends, which are subject to double taxation (taxed at both the corporate and individual income tax level, unless they qualify under "dividend exclusion").
- There's the potential for exposing the C corporation's assets to limited partnership liability, because the C corporation is the general partner in the limited partnership. Since the C corporation is the general partner in the limited partnership, and a general partner does not enjoy limited liability protection, the corporation's assets are potentially at risk from exposure to liabilities of the partnership.

When you combine a limited partnership and a C corporation, you have the benefits of a limited partnership plus the liability protection of having the C corporation substitute (for you) as the limited partnership's general partner.

CHAPTER 9

Limited Liability Company (LLC) Plus C Corporation

STRATEGY 32

Select a combination of a limited liability company (LLC) plus a C corporation form of business organization if you want to take profits out of your LLC (tax-free to you) and/or fund owner fringe benefits for yourself out of an LLC.

Under current tax law, you may elect to have your LLC taxed as a C corporation. Once this election is made, your business would operate as if it were a C corporation—without the biggest advantage of a C corporation (the ability to raise large sums of money through a public offering of the corporation's stock) and keeping the tax disadvantages of a C corporation.

Pay corporate tax, then receive a profit distribution in the form of dividends, which are subject to the dividend exclusion tax law.

The limited liability company (LLC) form of organization allows for multiple owners. Each is called a *member*. Members enjoy limited liability. There is also a *managing member* (in this instance, the C corporation) who is *not* personally liable for the financial obligations of the LLC. The members in the LLC are also the shareholders of the C corporation. The profits or losses of the LLC pass directly through to the owner's personal income tax return, Form 1040. The LLC files a Form 1065, and then lists each member's taxable profit on a Schedule K-1. *Note:* The C corporation also receives a Schedule K-1. The bottom-line profit of the LLC is *not* considered to be earned income to the members and is therefore *not* subject to self-employment tax.

The combination of a limited liability company (LLC) and a C corporation creates a situation whereby the C corporation becomes the managing member (owner) in the limited liability company (LLC). You are both a member (owner) in the LLC and a shareholder (owner) in the C corporation.

Advantages

- The limited liability company (LLC) can have as members (i.e., owners) both an individual and the C corporation simultaneously. You can structure your partnership such that both you, as an individual, and your C corporation, as a separate tax entity, can be members of the LLC. This allows you to take profit out of your partnership as well as to move cash into the C corporation, where it can be used to fund fringe benefits and other activities that are beneficial to you personally.
- The C corporation can be the managing member of the limited liability company (LLC). You can be the sole owner of the C corporation, and in that role you can make decisions for your LLC without having to assume the personal liability associated with being the managing member of your limited liability company (LLC).
- The individual member in the limited liability company can be the sole owner in the C corporation. You can enjoy the benefits of limited liability as a member of your LLC while you, as the sole owner of your C corporation (the managing member of your LLC), direct the activities of your LLC.
- The LLC can have as members (owners) both an individual and the C corporation simultaneously. As one of the members of your LLC, this allows you to structure an entity (the C corporation) that can accumulate cash at a beginning tax rate of 15 percent (which can be lower than yours) and that can serve as a framework offering fringe benefits to you, such as a retirement plan.
- The C corporation can be the managing member of your LLC. You can be the sole owner of the C corporation, and in that role you can make decisions for your LLC without having to personally assume the liability associated with being the managing member of your LLC.
- The individual can be a member in your LLC. As a member, you enjoy protection from LLC liability while enjoying the benefits of being able to profit directly from the activities of the LLC.
- The LLC can compensate its members, including your C corporation, using "distributions of profit." You and your C corporation are both members in the LLC, and as such can both receive distributions of profits from the LLC.

- There exists limited personal liability for the owners (members) of both the LLC and the C corporation. As the owner of an LLC and a C corporation, you enjoy the benefits of no exposure to the current or future liabilities of either entity.
- The LLC can compensate the individual member-owner using "guaranteed payments," which are considered "earned income" to the recipient. You can receive guaranteed payments from the LLC. This creates earned income for you, which qualifies you for fringe benefits, such as retirement plan participation.
- The LLC can compensate the C corporation using "consulting or management fees," which are considered income to the C corporation. Cash can be moved out of the LLC and into the C corporation. This cash can be then used to fund the activities of your C corporation.
- The C corporation can compensate owner(s) using wages, which are considered "earned income" to the recipient(s). You can take cash out of your C corporation and in the form of earned income by having your corporation pay you wages.
- The profit of LLC is *not* subject to self-employment tax, since it is not considered earned income. The bottom-line profit of the LLC is not considered earned income and is therefore exempt from self-employment tax, although each member's pro rata share of LLC profit does represent taxable income to the members.
- Any losses of the LLC can pass through to its owners' tax returns. The LLC can generate a loss (hopefully just a "paper loss" created by implementing tax strategies). Members can use their own pro rata share of any losses to offset other taxable income on their personal income tax returns.
- Profits of the LLC can be upstreamed to the C corporation, whereby these profits may enjoy lower tax rates. This can be accomplished by the payment of a "consulting or management fee" from the LLC to the C corporation and by the LLC making a "distribution of its profits" to the C corporation.
- Upstreamed profits can be sheltered by tax-deductible business expenses of the C corporation and provide "earned income," allowing the C corporation to use this earned income as the basis for qualified retirement plan(s) for its wage-earning employees.
- The LLC members' (owners') pro rata share of profits represent taxable income to the C corporation (managing member), whether or not they are distributed. Profits can be upstreamed to the C corporation, whether or not they are actually distributed (in full or in part). The corporation's pro rata share of the LLC's bottom-line profit is automatically upstreamed to the corporation for tax purposes.
- The C corporation can compensate its shareholders using wages, which are considered "earned income to the recipient." As the shareholder of a C corporation, if you

Table 9.1   Computing Excludable Dividend Amount (EDA)

Dollar amount of the	
C corporation's taxable income	$100,000
Using a 34% corporate income tax rate	× .34
Dollar amount of U.S. tax due	$ 34,000
Dollar amount of the	
C corporation's taxable income	$100,000
Dollar amount of U.S. tax due	($ 34,000)
Excludable dividend amount (EDA)	$ 66,000

work in the business you are allowed to pay yourself a fair and reasonable wage for work you perform. This wage or salary (W-2 wage) is considered earned income to you. This earned income allows you to qualify for fringe benefits, such as your participation in a retirement plan, based on earned income.

- You are subject to the dividend exclusion. When a C corporation pays dividends to its shareholders, these dividends are paid out of after-tax profits (after corporate profits have been paid). However, under the dividend exclusion tax laws, a portion of the C corporation's after-tax profits can be distributed to shareholders in the form of dividends, which are tax-free to the shareholder recipients. This share of C corporation profits is called the *excludable dividend amount*. The formula for determining the EDA, in example form is shown in Table 9.1. Under the scenario in Table 9.1, this C corporation could pay a tax-free dividend to its shareholders.

Disadvantages

- The owners' pro rata share of profits represents taxable income to the general partner (the C corporation) and to any limited partners, whether or not they are distributed. This means that partners can have tax liability for profits they did receive, as well as profits they never received (i.e., the portion of the limited partnership profits that were not distributed).
- Owners are limited to two ways of taking compensation out of the corporation: Shareholders of a C corporation can either pay themselves W-2 wages, which are subject to both self-employment tax and income tax (at the owner's personal income tax rate), or they can pay themselves dividends, which are subject to double taxation

(taxed at both the corporate and individual income tax level, unless they qualify under "dividend exclusion").

Remember, by having the C corporation as the managing member of your LLC, you can double your personal liability protection while simultaneously enjoying the tax benefits of both an LLC and a C corporation.

Your Persona

There are several major ways you can convert personal expenditures into tax-deductible business expenses. Part 2 covers these deductions. The information and strategies in this section focus on items such as your home, your car, and other personal expenditures that can have a business (as well as a personal) purpose. I lump these together as "Your Persona." Once you have chosen the form of business organization that minimizes taxes, you can use this section to further minimize your business's income tax liability.

Part 2 consists of the following chapters:

A significant portion of your personal life—or as I call it, "Your Persona"—can be positively affected by owning your own business. Tax deductions may involve the items and activities that, although personal in nature, become an integral part of your business when you "make your life tax deductible." These items and activities include your home, your car, your equipment (e.g., computers), your travel and entertainment, your family, and yourself. (*Note:* Also included is your retirement, which is covered in depth in Part 3 of this book.)

The dollars you are currently spending on these items are personal in nature. After you pay your personal (Form 1040) income taxes, you can spend the remaining after-tax dollars on items and activities that are personal in nature.

However, if you are a business owner, many of these items and activities become tax deductible. This means that before you pay any taxes, you can spend dollars on these (formerly "personal") items and activities that have now become tax-deductible business expenses. The items and activities that make up your persona are discussed in this part of the book.

CHAPTER 10

Your Home

As a small-business owner, you may qualify to take a home office tax deduction (IRS Form 8829). In order to qualify for the deduction, your form of business organization must be noncorporate, and the use of your home office must be both "exclusive" and "regular." *Noncorporate* means that your form of business organization must be something other than that of a corporation. Acceptable noncorporate forms of business organization for a home office deduction are a sole proprietorship, a partnership, a limited partnership, a one-member LLC (taxed as a sole proprietorship), and a multiple-member LLC (taxed as a partnership).

If you qualify, you may deduct certain other expenditures, such as depreciation and the indirect expenses of operating your home, on a pro rata basis. Even if you fail to qualify for the home office deduction, you are allowed to deduct other business expenses that you incur while operating your business out of your home.

STRATEGY 33

Qualify to take your home office tax deduction.

Qualifying to take a home office deduction is a two-step process.

Step 1. You must be using a portion of your home for your business, and you must be doing so on both an exclusive and a regular basis. For clarification, here are some definitions to follow as guidelines:

- *Exclusive use.* You must use a separate area of your home (or a separate unattached structure) *only* for your business. This area can be a room or other separately identifiable space, although the space does not need to be marked off by a permanent partition. *Note:* If you use an area for both personal and business purposes (e.g., space for storage of inventory, a day care facility), you do not need to meet the requirements of the exclusive test; however, you are required to prorate the total space between personal and business use to identify the business portion.

- *Regular use.* You must use a specific area of your home for business on a continuing basis. *Note:* You do not meet this test if your business use of the area is only occasional or incidental—even if you do not use that area for any other purpose.

Step 2. The business part of your home must be *one* of the following locations:

- Your principal place of business. Your home office will qualify as your principal place of business if *both* of the following conditions are met:
    1. You must use it exclusively and regularly for administrative and management activities of your business.
    2. You must have no other fixed location where you conduct substantial administrative or management activities of your business.

Note that you can have more than one business location, including your home, for a single business. If you do, and your home office does not qualify as your principal place of business based on the previous two conditions, you should determine your principal place of business as follows:

1. Evaluate relative importance of the activities performed at each location.
2. If the relative importance factor does not determine your principal place of business, you can consider the time spent at each location.

- A place where you meet or deal directly with patients, clients, or customers in the normal course of your business.
- A separate structure (not attached to your home) that you use in connection with your business.

You either qualify for a home office deduction or you do not. There is no partial qualification available. If you qualify for a home office deduction, you can use the information in Table 10.1 to calculate your deduction on a pro rata basis. To determine how much of your home you use exclusively for your business, divide your home office square footage by the total square footage of your total home. This gives you the percentage of your home that you use (exclusively) as a home office. Use this percentage to prorate your total home expenses (depreciation and indirect expenses), listed in Table 10.1.

Table 10.1   Calculating your home office deduction on a pro rata basis.

1. Depreciation calculation on the allowable home office

   The cost basis of the house: this equals the lower of the ($) cost
   of the property (excluding the cost of the land), or the fair market
   value of the house at the time it was first used for business, plus
   the cost of improvements that are made over time. $XXX

   Approximately 3.175% per year (see depreciation tables for exact
   figures based on 39 years).   × $XXX

   The annual depreciation amount (prior to your prorating this figure
   to reflect the percentage of business use). $XXX

2. "Indirect expenses" that apply to business use (on a proportionate basis)
   a. our home mortgage interest
   b. Real property taxes on your home

      Note: Items deducted as home office deductions cannot be deducted
      as Schedule A itemized deductions.

   c. Insurance
   d. Rent
   e. Utilities (heat and light)
   f. Wages for domestic help
   g. Local telephone service (excluding your basic service)

STRATEGY 34

**Deduct the cost of "ordinary and necessary" business expenditures—
even if your home office doesn't qualify for the home office tax
deduction.**

Even if you don't qualify for the home office deduction, you are nonetheless allowed
to deduct the following "ordinary and necessary" business expenses that apply specifi-

cally to your business and any direct expenses that you incur exclusively for your home office.

- Professional services: accounting, attorney, consultant
- Logistical support: alarm services; online services; dues and subscriptions; rent, cleaning, utilities, telephone equipment, local and long-distance telephone service (*caution:* no deduction for the first phone line into your home), office supplies; postage, freight, and shipping; printing; repairs and maintenance
- Financial: bank service charges, interest expense, commissions
- Office expenses (e.g., outside rent and home office expenses)
- Travel
- Your car

    Your business can take the number of business miles driven using a specific car multiplied by 48.5 cents per mile, and you can do so every year.

    Your business can deduct all the actual expenses of owning and operating a specific car for business purposes.

    The actual cost of the car, applicable to business use, is deducted over five years using regular and bonus depreciation methods and Section 179. (For more about your car, see Chapter 11.)

- Equipment and furniture and fixtures (deducted over seven years)
- Real estate (deducted over 39 years)
- Entertainment
- Funding your retirement
- Hiring your family
- Tax-free owner benefits (e.g., company cars, long-term care, and life insurance)
- Wages and salaries
- Retirement plan contributions
- Employee benefits (e.g., child care, education, and adoption)
- Marketing
- Business insurance
- Medical health insurance (for the business owners and employees)
- Payroll taxes
- Other taxes (e.g., sales taxes)
- Start-up and organizational expenditures incurred after 10/22/04

    Under $5,000—expensed in the year incurred
    In excess of $5,000—deducted over 60 months

STRATEGY 35

Take the following precautions when you deduct your home office.

---

1. You cannot take home office deductions that create a loss during a current tax year. Once your home office deductions zero out your income, any unused portion of the current year's home office deductions can be carried forward—until the "loss carryforward" dollar amount is fully used up as a tax deduction.
2. If your home office is used for more than one business, you must meet the home office tests for all your businesses before you claim a home office deduction. If one or more business fails to qualify, the IRS will disallow your home office tax deduction *entirely.*
3. If you take a home office deduction (e.g., allocating 10 percent of the cost of your home as a home office deduction), remember that when you sell your home, 10 percent (in this example) of the gain on the sale of your home will be subject to capital gains tax. The balance of the gain on the sale of your home can be excluded from capital gains tax—up to $250,000 in gain if you are single ($500,000 if you are married)—provided that you (and your spouse, if married) lived in your home as your principal residence for at least two of the preceding five years (before the sale).

When you are using a noncorporate form of business organization, you are entitled to deduct your home office as well as all other allowable business expenditures.

CHAPTER **11**

Your Car

If you use your car in your business, you can deduct the costs of operating and maintaining your car (but *only* that portion pertaining to business). This is accomplished by allocating the total cost of operating and maintaining your car between deductible business use and nondeductible personal use. Business costs can be deducted by using either actual costs or the standard mileage rate.

STRATEGY 36

Deduct local transportation expenses when using your car for business purposes.

Costs associated with the business use of your car are divided into two categories.

1. *Local transportation (within your tax home) and overnight travel (outside of your tax home).* Your *tax home* is defined as your regular place of business (regardless of where you maintain your family home). It includes the entire city or general area in which your business is located. The following are considered deductible car-related local transportation expenses:

   • Getting from one workplace to another in the course of your business when you are traveling within the city or general area that is your tax home
   • Visiting clients or customers
   • Going to a business meeting away from your regular workplace

- Getting from your home to a temporary workplace when you have one or more regular places of work within your tax home

2. *Overnight travel expenses, including the costs of traveling away from your tax home overnight.* Note that the expenses you incur getting from your home to a temporary workplace when you have one or more regular places of work outside your tax home are also fully deductible.

STRATEGY 37

Convert a portion of your car to business use.

You can deduct business use through either of two methods: the standard mileage rate or actual expenses. (See Table 11.1 for a summary of each.)

Table 11.1   Summary of the Two Methods of Deducting the Cost of Operating Your Car for Business Year 1

Method 1: Standard mileage rate = 48.5 cents × number of business miles

Total miles driven	18,750
Less personal miles driven	−4,230
Business miles driven	14,520
Standard mileage rate	× $ .485
Deduction for business use of your car	$7,042

Note: The calculation of the deduction is the same regardless of the curb weight of your car, which is typically shown by the manufacturer on the inside of the driver's side door and is applicable for *actual expenses* (method 2).

Percentage of business use = business miles ÷ total miles

$$77\% = \frac{14,520}{18,750}$$

Table 11.1   (*Continued*)

Method 2: Actual expenses

	Three examples using different curb weights		
Example	1	2	3
Curb weight of car (in pounds)	≤6,000	6,000–14,000	14,000+
Cost of the car	$50,000	$85,000	$120,000
Less Sec. 179 max.	$ 0	($25,000)	($105,000)
Balance to depreciate	$50,000	$60,000	$ 15,000
Less special depreciation @ 50% (1)	($25,000)	($30,000)	($ 7,500)
Balance to depreciate	$25,000	$30,000	$ 7,500
Less regular depreciation @ 20% (2)	($ 5,000)	($ 6,000)	($ 1,500)
Total calculated depreciation (1 + 2)	$30,000	$36,000	$ 9,000
Total (maximum) allowable year 1 depreciation	$10,710	$10,710	$ 10,710
Sec. 179 max.	+$ 0	+$25,000	+$105,000
Total allowable year 1 cost of car deduction	$10,710	$35,710	$114,010
Total other actual costs of operating your car, year 1 (gas, ins., oil, repairs, etc.)	+$ 6,688	+$ 8,421	+$ 15,679
Total actual expenses allowed, assuming 100% business use	$17,398	$44,131	$129,679
Times 77% business use	× .77	× .77	× .77
Total allowable year 1 car deduction	$13,396	$33,981	$ 99,853

1. Standard mileage rate
   - Depreciation is built into the rate, so don't depreciate your car when using the standard mileage rate.
   - The standard mileage rate is 48.5 cents per mile. This rate applies for a car, van, pickup, or panel truck.
2. Actual expenses
   - These are prorated based on the percentage of business miles divided by total miles plus depreciation.

Some rules of thumb for standard mileage rate are as follows:

- When using the standard mileage rate for a year, you *cannot* deduct your actual expenses for that year, except for business-related parking fees and tolls.
- For a car you own: If you want to use the standard mileage rate for a car (or truck) you own, you must choose to use it in the first year the car is put into service in your business; in later years, you can choose to use either the standard mileage rate or actual expenses.
- For a car you lease: If you want to use the standard mileage rate for a car lease, you must choose to use it for the entire lease period.
- You cannot use the standard mileage rate if you operate two or more cars (for business use) at the same time.

Actual car expenses include the following:

Garage rent
Gas
Insurance
Interest
Licenses
Oil
Parking fees
Registration fees
Repairs
Tires and tolls
The cost of the car

- If you own your car, recover its cost by deducting allowable depreciation expense.
- If you lease your car, recover its cost by deducting its monthly lease payments (prorate between business and personal use).

Note: If you lease a car with a fair market value over $15,500, you will have to report (as income) an amount based on IRS calculations. This income rule applies if you deduct the business portion of your lease payments plus other operating costs; it does *not* apply if you claim the standard mileage allowance.

The income inclusion amount reduces the deduction for lease payments, so that it equals the amount that would be deductible as depreciation if the car had been bought outright. The income amount is reduced (1) if the car was leased for less than the entire year or (2) if the business use is less than 100 percent.

STRATEGY 38

Calculate your car deduction using both the standard rate and actual expenses, and then select the method that gives you the larger tax deduction.

If you qualify to use either the standard mileage rate or actual expenses, calculate your deduction both ways to see which method gives you the larger deduction.

There are four factors you should consider in making your choice between the standard mileage rate and actual expenses:

1. Total miles you drive
2. Business miles you drive
3. The cost of your vehicle
4. Actual expenses incurred

You may switch from standard mileage rates to the actual expense method. (You don't have to reduce the depreciable basis of the car by the depreciation built into the standard rate (X business miles taken) before calculating the new depreciation expense deduction). To take full advantage of this, you should maintain a daily mileage log for every car you use for business purposes.

STRATEGY 39

Deduct the actual cost of driving your car for business purposes, using one of the two allowable depreciation methods for deducting your car.

Two depreciation methods are available for your car. Table 11.2 illustrates the percentage deduction for these.

1. *Modified accelerated cost recovery system (MACRS).* This is typically preferred when business use is more than 50 percent, then changed to straight line when that method yields a larger deduction.
2. *Straight-line method.* This is *required* when business use is less than 50 percent, but can also be used when business use is more than 50 percent.

Table 11.2   Depreciation Methods, Percentage Deductions

Year	MACRS	Straight Line	Luxury Limit
1	20.00%	10.00%	$10,710
2	32.00%	20.00%	
3	19.20%	20.00%	
4	11.52%	20.00%	
5	11.52%	20.00%	
6	5.76%	10.00%	

STRATEGY 40

Watch out for the impact of the alternative minimum tax when using MACRS depreciation to deduct your car.

Accelerated depreciation (MACRS) is subject to alternative minimum tax. If you elect to use the MACRS depreciation method in expensing the cost of business use for your car, you may be liable for additional income tax when you sell your car. The IRS allows you to choose a depreciation method (like MACRS) whereby you may deduct the cost of your car (if used for business purposes) much more quickly. If you use straight-line depreciation, for example, the cost of business use for your car will be spread out over a longer period of time (i.e., more years). MACRS speeds up the process of writing off your car.

However, when you sell your car, you may be required to recapture the dollar amount of the depreciation difference between the faster MACRS method and the slower straight-line method. Under the alternative minimum tax rules, this means you may be required to pay tax on this difference. Hopefully, if you elect to use the MACRS method, the additional annual tax savings will more than offset the depreciation recapture tax due.

STRATEGY 41

Determine the percentage of business use for your car using a mileage log.

The percentage of business use is determined from your mileage log. Take the actual miles driven for business during a given tax year (as recorded in your car's business mileage log). You should keep a log continuously for all the driving you do, showing all business miles driven, all personal miles driven, and the total miles driven during a given tax year (the 12-month tax year applicable to your business's form of organization). Then simply divide the number of business miles by the total miles your car was driven that tax year. This will give you the percentage of time that your car was used for business.

For example, if you drove your car 14,520 miles on business (out of 18,750 total miles driven) during a given tax year, the percentage of business use applicable to your car would be 14,520 divided by 18,750, or 77 percent. You used your car 77 percent of the time on business. This means that you are allowed to deduct 77 percent of all the applicable annual costs of operating your car (including its original purchase price).

STRATEGY 42

Calculate your business's depreciation tax deduction for business use of your car.

There are six steps in the process of calculating your business's depreciation expense tax deduction for business use of your car:

Step 1. Determine the depreciation cost basis of your car (this could be the purchase price plus such costs, such as sales tax, or minus special sales incentives, such as cash rebates).

Step 2. Select a depreciation method.

Step 3. Determine the depreciation percentage for the specific tax year in the tax life of the car (e.g., year 1) used under the depreciation method you selected.

Step 4. Apply the depreciation percentage you selected to the depreciation cost basis of your car to determine the total potential depreciation expense tax deduction for your car for the tax year in question.

Step 5. Determine the percentage of business use applicable to your car.

Step 6. Apply the percentage of business use to the total potential depreciation expense to determine the allowable tax deduction for business use of your car.

Here is an example:

Step 1. $50,000
Step 2. Straight-line method
Step 3. 20%
Step 4. $50,000 × 20% = $10,000
Step 5. 14,520 miles ÷ 18,750 = 77%
Step 6. 77% × $10,000 = $7,700

Note: This is well within the annual maximum depreciation expense tax deduction for a car in the year of acquisition (year 1) of $10,710. This is called the annual *luxury limit* for cars.

STRATEGY 43

Deduct the cost of more than one car, when applicable.

If you already have two vehicles, rather than using one exclusively for business (the IRS is skeptical when you claim that a personal car is used 100 percent for business), maintain a daily mileage log, keeping business miles separate, and then you can deduct a portion of both cars for business use.

Deducting a portion of both cars generally provides a greater deduction than claiming 100 percent of one car. *Note:* This is applicable whether you use actual expenses or the standard mileage rate.

STRATEGY 44

When changing vehicles, select the tax treatment that maximizes your tax advantage.

No gain or loss is recognized on a trade-in of a car used 100 percent for business use.

When disposing of your current car, use the following format to determine the gain (or loss) on the sale of a vehicle:

> Original cost
> −Depreciation
> Adjusted basis
> −Proceeds from the sale of the vehicle
> Gain (or loss) on the sale

For example:

> $45,000 (original cost)
> −$30,000 (depreciation)
> $15,000 (adjusted basis)
> −$10,000 (proceeds from the sale of the vehicle)
> ($5,000) (loss on the sale)

1. Sell vehicles that produce deductible losses (and take the loss in the year of the sale).
2. Trade vehicles that produce taxable profits. When you trade your old vehicle for a newer one, you take the old adjusted basis and add any cash received to determine the new basis for depreciation. This trade defers the gain over the life of the new vehicle.

STRATEGY 45

Choose buying over leasing—based on the after-tax cost.

The after-tax cost of leasing is generally 10 to 20 percent more than the cost of purchasing. This provides profit to the leasing company. Should you decide to lease a car for more than 30 days, and the fair market of the car at the beginning of the lease was more than $15,500, you may be required to report as income an amount based on the IRS inclusion tables (for leased cars). This inclusion amount can be anywhere from $1 to in excess of $3000, depending on the fair market value of the car, the tax year of the lease (one to five or more years in the lease), and the year in which the lease originated. This inclusion amount is designed to reduce the deduction for monthly lease payments so that it equals the amount that would be deductible as depreciation if the car had been bought outright.

Income inclusion applies if you deduct the business portion of your lease payments plus other operating expenses; it does not apply if you claim the standard mileage allowance of 48.5 cents per business mile driven.

The major decision that you must make in making your car tax deductible is which of the two methods you should use: (1) the standard mileage rate (48.5 cents per business mile) or (2) actuals, where all the costs of owning and maintaining your car are prorated between personal and business use.

CHAPTER 12

Your Equipment

Equipment can become tax deductible to your business in two ways: (1) when you convert your personal equipment into business equipment by contributing it to your business, and (2) when your business purchases and places equipment into service.

STRATEGY 46

Make your equipment, furniture, and fixtures tax deductible.

It is possible to deduct your equipment, furniture, and fixtures one of two ways:

1. *Convert personal assets into business deductions when they are used in your business.* As a sole proprietor (or one-member LLC), you can convert these assets merely by using them for business purposes. In a partnership, limited partnership, limited liability company (LLC), or corporation (S or C), you can convert personal equipment as a portion of your investment in the business or by using a loan.
2. *Purchase and place into service equipment and/or furniture and fixtures to make them tax deductible during the current tax year.* Once this has occurred, you can elect either to depreciate the item(s) or expense them as assets using Section 179. This allows you to expense the cost of equipment (which has been purchased and placed into service in your business) up to $105,000 per year. Note that in order for equipment to qualify under Section 179, the equipment must be purchased, not converted from your personal asset into a business asset.

Note: As a way of reducing the paperwork associated with expensing smaller contributed or purchased assets that are used by your business, it is recommended that any asset costing less than $100 be written off in full in the tax year in which it is purchased. If its cost is higher than $100, you can elect to either depreciate it or asset-expense it using Section 179.

The depreciable basis of property used in business is determined by its value at the time it is placed in service. If it is new, then use the purchase price; if it is already owned, then use its fair market value at that time.

STRATEGY 47

Depreciate the cost of your equipment, furniture, and fixtures.

Equipment, furniture, and fixtures are considered seven-year property and are depreciated over an eight-year period. Some common examples of furniture and fixtures are desks and files, cellular phones, and fax machines.

These items are to be depreciated using either the seven-year MACRS (accelerated), or the MACRS straight-line depreciation methods. Notice that the MACRS accelerated methods allow you to deduct the asset faster than the corresponding straight-line method. Use Table 12.1 to calculate the proper percentage rate applicable to your particular depreciable asset.

Table 12.1	Depreciation Rates for Seven-Year Property	
Year	**MACRS**	**Straight-Line Method**
1	14.29%	7.14%
2	24.49%	14.29%
3	17.49%	14.29%
4	12.49%	14.28%
5	8.93%	14.29%
6	8.92%	14.28%
7	8.93%	14.29%
8	4.46%	7.14%

STRATEGY 48

Use Section 179 to accelerate the pace of deducting your equipment, furniture, and fixtures.

Any depreciable asset that you purchase and place into service in your business can be expensed using Section 179 *asset expensing*. Under Section 179, you are allowed to deduct the cost of assets that qualify for Section 179 up to the current limit of $105,000 per tax year.

Any remaining portion of an asset's cost that is not expensed under Section 179 can then be depreciated, using your choice of appropriate depreciation methods, over the indicated number of years going forward. There are three key things to be aware of, however, if you plan to do this:

1. To qualify for Section 179 asset expensing, an asset's percentage of business use must exceed a 50 percent threshold in the year the item is first placed into service. If the business use falls to 50 percent or less after the year the properties were placed in service, but before the end of the depreciable recovery period, you must *recapture* (i.e., reverse) the benefit from the first-year expense deduction.
2. Your asset expense deduction may not exceed the net taxable income of your business.
3. If the total cost of the qualifying property placed in service during a taxable year is more than $400,000, the annual $105,000 expensing limit is reduced (dollar for dollar) by the dollar amount by which the qualifying property exceeds the $400,000 limit.

STRATEGY 49

Take advantage of the special 50 percent bonus depreciation allowance.

A special depreciation allowance is available for new property acquired and placed into service after May 5, 2003. The 50 percent depreciation allowance is figured on the adjusted basis after taking any Section 179 deduction. The adjusted basis is then reduced by the 50 percent depreciation allowance before calculating the regular depreciation deduction for the first year and all subsequent tax years.

Following is a comparison of the three options (allowed by the IRS) available to you when you take a first-year deduction on your business equipment. Included are examples of how you could deduct the cost of equipment ($80,000 and $110,000, respectively) under that option.

Option 1. Take Section 179.

Cost of equipment (in $)	80,000	110,000
Less Sec. 179 deduction allowed	−80,000	−105,000 (Sec. 179 upper limit)
Balance to be depreciated (over future years)	0	5,000

Option 2. *Don't* take Section 179, but *do* take special depreciation allowance; then take regular depreciation to the extent allowed.

Cost of equipment (in $)	80,000	110,000
Less Sec. 179	0	0
Balance to be depreciated	80,000	110,000
Less special depreciation allowance @50%	−40,000	−55,000
Deduction allowed due to the special depreciation allowance	40,000	55,000
Remaining depreciable basis	40,000	55,000
Regular MACRS depreciation @ 20%	+8,000	+11,000
Special depreciation (see above @50%)	+40,000	55,000
Total deduction allowed	$48,000	$66,000
Balance to be depreciated (over future years)	$32,000	$44,000

Option 3. *Don't* take Section 179, *don't* take special depreciation allowance, but *do* take regular depreciation.

Cost of equipment (in $)	80,000	110,000
Less Sec. 179	0	0
Balance to be depreciated	80,000	110,000
Less special depreciation allowance @50%	0	0
Balance to be depreciated	80,000	110,000
Less regular depreciation @ 20%	16,000	22,000
Total deduction allowed	$16,000	$22,000
Balance to be depreciated (over future years)	$64,000	$88,000

STRATEGY 50

Depreciate the cost of equipment, furniture, and fixtures based on business use.

Determine the percentage of personal/business use of equipment, furniture, and fixtures and then apply this percentage to Section 179 asset expensing, special bonus depreciation allowance, and regular depreciation using these two steps:

Step 1. Calculate the percentage of business use. For example, divide the number of days of business use by the total number of days available, say 270 days of business use divided by 360 total number of days available in a year (270 ÷ 360 = 75% business use). A 90-day log of typical usage of each item provides a written record.

Step 2. Use the following formula to determine the applicable depreciation deduction for the particular item in question:

Your basis in the property = cost of the property when put in service + improvements × applicable depreciation % based on the method used = tentative depreciation deduction ($) × calculated % of business use (see step 1) = your ($) depreciation deduction

---

STRATEGY 51

When deducting the purchase cost of equipment, furniture, and fixtures, use the depreciation method that best matches maximum depreciation deductions against the maximum amount of taxable business income.

As a business owner, you have a number of different depreciation methods from which to choose. Some of them deduct the cost of equipment and furniture and fixtures by creating a depreciation expense each year (in the official IRS predetermined "useful life" of the equipment or property) that is about the same dollar amount. This spreads the depreciation expense evenly over a specific number of years.

Other depreciation methods accelerate the rate at which the cost is deducted. These are called *accelerated depreciation methods;* MACRS is one of these. Your goal should be to take the greater depreciation deduction during the years for which your business's profit (and therefore its *marginal tax rate,* or the tax rate applicable to the last dollar of your business profit) is highest and to take a lesser amount of depreciation expense when your business's profit is lower. In this manner, you will be reducing your business's taxable income when it is at its highest and likely at a higher marginal tax rate. Be aware that MACRS (accelerated depreciation) is subject to the alternative minimum tax (ATM); this means that if you elect to use the MACRS depreciation method in expensing the cost of your business equipment, you may be liable for additional income tax (under depreciation recapture rules) when you sell the equipment.

Deducting the cost of your business equipment requires that you use depreciation as a way of writing off the cost of the equipment over its useful life (as determined by the IRS). Also, don't forget Section 179 as a way to deduct up to $105,000 annually in equipment purchases.

CHAPTER 13

Your Travel and Entertainment

Travel expenses can be incurred when you are away from home for business purposes. You are considered to be traveling away from home if *both* the following conditions are met:

1. Your duties require you to be away from the general area of your tax home substantially longer than an ordinary day's work.
2. You need to get sleep or rest to meet the demands of your work while away from home.

The Internal Revenue Service's definition of tax-deductible *entertainment expenses* include the expenses associated with any activity generally considered to provide entertainment, amusement, or recreation. These include entertaining business guests at nightclubs; at social, athletic, and sporting events; at theaters; on yachts; during hunting, fishing, and other vacations; or even sending a car to customers or their families.

STRATEGY 52

Deduct 100 percent of your business travel expenses.

Here are some typical travel-related expenses:

- *Transportation.* Travel by airplane, train, bus, or car between your home and your business destination—if the principal purpose of the trip is business.

- *Taxi, commuter bus, and airport limousine.* Fares that take you to or from the airport or station and your hotel, or between the hotel and the work location of your customer's or client's business meeting.
- *Baggage and shipping.* Sending baggage and sample or display material to and from your regular work location and your travel business site.
- *Car.* Operating and maintaining your car when traveling away from home on business. You can use the actual expense method or the standard mileage rate. Include business-related tolls and parking. If you rent a car while away from home on business, you can deduct the business-use portion of the rental expenses.
- *Lodging.* Your lodging is deductible if your business trip is overnight or long enough that you need to stop for sleep or rest to properly perform your duties.
- *Meals.* You can deduct 50 percent of the cost of meals if it is necessary that you stop for sleep or rest to properly perform your duties. This includes the cost of the meal, tax, and tips.
- *Cleaning.* Dry cleaning and laundry expenses you incur *while* traveling on business are deductible.
- *Telephone.* Business calls while on your business trip are deductible; this includes telephone credit card calls, hotel and pay phone charges, mobile phones, and fax transmissions.
- *Temporary office expenses.* These include such expenses as renting computer access or printing/photocopy services.
- *Tips.* Tips related to the services in this list.
- *Other.* Ordinary and necessary expenses related to your business travel may include transportation to and from a business meal, computer and other equipment rentals, and even rental space for meetings.

STRATEGY 53

Allocate travel expenses between business and nonbusiness.

Identify business expenses that are tax deductible. If your travel is all business, you can deduct all the travel-related expenses. If your travel is part business, identify business-related expenses and separate them from the cost of your extended stay at your business destination, a nonbusiness side trip, or other nonbusiness activities. The best way to accomplish the splitting up of business and non-business-related expenditures is to create and maintain a travel log.

You will find it rather easy to include personal time in conjunction with your business travel. In this manner, you will virtually never have to take completely non-tax-deductible personal trips; rather, combine your personal trips with your business trips and convert what would have been personal airfare into 100 percent tax-deductible business airfare. When your personal trips become mostly business travel, the tax savings are tremendous.

STRATEGY 54

Do not prorate the travel costs to and from your business destination.

You are not required to prorate the travel costs of getting to and from your business destination. For example, if you fly to and from your business destination, the entire cost of these tickets (airplane, train, car, bus, boat, etc.) is 100 percent tax deductible to your business—even if you engage in nonbusiness activities while on your business trip. As long as the principal purpose of the trip is business, you can always deduct the cost of your round-trip.

One of the best examples of the application of this tax law is if you were to travel to and from the Hawaiian Islands for business. Even though the dollar cost of the round-trip airfare would typically represent a very significant portion of your overall travel expenditures, you can write it off completely as a tax-deductible business expense.

STRATEGY 55

Qualify your days as "business days."

You can qualify a day for business (and therefore for a business tax deduction) if your primary activity was business. A good rule of thumb is that your business activity should be at least four hours in length during normal working hours.

This allows you to convert a substantial part of what would have been business time into time that you can enjoy playing, not working. The definition of *business day* is very liberal, and for that reason, personal and family time while you're on business can actually be much greater than business time. For example, consider a 24-hour day: even if you spend 10 hours sleeping, dressing, and eating in addition to your 4 hours of business, you still have another 10 hours for fun.

The significance of this strategy cannot be overstated when you travel with your family. For example, if you were traveling to a resort to attend a business conference, your family could accompany you, enjoy the resort activities, and you could still qualify *your* days as business days.

STRATEGY 56

Deduct travel expenses for another individual who travels with you on a business trip.

You can deduct the travel expenses for another individual who travels with you on a business trip under three scenarios.

1. The individual is part owner of your business.
2. The individual is an employee of your business.
3. The individual is a business associate with whom it is reasonable to expect that you will actively conduct business:

   Customer
   Client
   Supplier
   Agent
   Partner (co-owner of the business)
   Professional adviser

This means that you can take individuals with you and deduct 100 percent of their business travel as long as they are directly associated with your business in any one of the preceding three circumstances. This broadens the definition of business travel to include others around you—as long as they are on a business purpose as well.

This tax law was redefined after years of business owners taking a friend, a spouse, or another family member (such as children) along with them on business trips and deducting their travel expenditures—even though their presence on the trip was clearly not related to business. However, as is often the case, when the IRS clarified the tax law, it paved the way for deducting the cost of travel for the very same individuals—as long as it is tied to ownership, employment, or the legitimate potential for generating new sales for your business. If your spouse is either a part owner or an employee, if your children are legitimate employees (paid for doing actual business work), and/or your friend has the ability to generate additional sales for your business (as perhaps either a customer or an agent of a customer), you are allowed to take the cost of their travel as a business deduction.

STRATEGY 57

Make weekends tax deductible when you travel.

Deduct weekends by sandwiching your weekend traveling with both a Friday and a Monday morning meeting. This is a very popular strategy; however, your success in deducting the travel cost of weekends in between business activities rests on your ability to substantiate your claim that there was legitimate and formal business activity on both Friday and Monday. If you are attending formal training or a seminar, this becomes automatic. However, if your business purpose on Friday is "official," but your business activity on Monday is more "unofficial," you might have difficulty justifying a tax deduction for the costs of the weekend in between. If you use common sense in applying this rule, your tax savings will be both significant and unchallenged.

One additional requirement in your justification for deducting these weekends in between business activities is that the costs directly associated with your staying at your business destination for the weekend must be less than the cost of returning home and then back again to the very same business destination for your Monday business activity.

STRATEGY 58

Deduct the cost of travel associated with attending a business convention.

You can deduct your travel expenses when you attend a convention if you can show that your attendance benefits your business. Proving that the convention benefits your business is open to a somewhat broad interpretation. The convention topics and content should include the following types of topics:

- Training related to product knowledge about your business's products and/or services
- Education on business-related topics (e.g., employee management, production techniques, accounting and bookkeeping, tax strategies)
- Sales training and development
- Business funding (loans and grants)
- Other business-related topics

The convention or seminar must have activities scheduled for a minimum of six hours during the day, and you must attend at least two-thirds of those activities, for a minimum of four hours per day.

Remember, you cannot deduct the travel expenses of your family members unless they are either part owners or employees of your business.

STRATEGY 59

Deduct costs associated with travel outside of the United States.

Deduct the entire cost of your travel outside of the United States—even if you do not spend your entire time on business activities—if you meet any one of the following three conditions. *Note:* Even if you do not spend your entire time outside of the United States on business activities, your travel is considered entirely for business, and you can deduct *all* of your business-related travel expenses . . . *if* you meet any one of the following conditions:

1. If you are outside the United States no more than one week (seven consecutive days)
2. If you are outside of the United States and less than 25 percent of the time was spent on nonbusiness (personal) activities
3. If you can establish that a personal vacation was *not* a major consideration, even if you have substantial control over arranging the travel

---

STRATEGY 60

Allocate the cost of travel outside the United States between business and nonbusiness.

Travel outside the United States does not have to be either totally business or totally nonbusiness. To maximize your deductible expenses, allocate business and nonbusiness expenses on the basis of the percentage of time you spent on business.

This can be calculated by dividing the number of business days by the total number of days you are in travel. Days are considered business days when they fall into one of the following four categories:

1. *Transportation days.* These include any days you spend traveling to or from a business destination. However, if because of a nonbusiness activity you do not travel by a direct route, your business days are the days it would take you to travel a reasonably direct route to your business destination. *Note:* Extra days for side trips or nonbusiness activities cannot be counted as business days.
2. *Presence required.* Count as a business day any day your presence is required at a particular place for a specific business purpose, even if you spent most of the day on nonbusiness activities.
3. *Days spent on business.* If your principal activity during working hours is pursuit of your business activities, count the day as a business day. Also, count as a business day any day you are prevented from working because of circumstances beyond your control.
4. *Certain weekends and holidays.* Count weekends and holidays and other necessary standby days as business days if they fall between business days. However, if they follow your business meetings or activity and you remain at your business destination for nonbusiness purposes, do not count them as business days.

STRATEGY 61

Deduct up to $2000 each year for attending cruise ship conventions that are directly related to your business.

You are allowed to take the cruise ship business deduction if you comply with all of the following conditions:

- The convention on board the ship must be business-related.
- The ship must be registered in the United States.
- All ports must be in the United States or one of its possessions.
- You must submit two supporting statements with your tax return.
- You must spend at least 51 percent of your (waking) time attending the seminar.

STRATEGY 62

Create and maintain a travel log.

The most important supporting documentation that you can create to justify deducting your travel expenditures is a travel log. This log should be maintained *contemporaneously* (meaning "as you go"). Do not try to reconstruct the log at the end of the tax year or, worse yet, years later when the IRS asks for it.

This travel log should include all business and non-business-related travel. In this manner, you will have no trouble differentiating between business and personal travel—especially for mixed-use travel that includes both deductible business expenditures and nondeductible personal travel expenditures.

If you properly maintain a travel log, you will never have trouble justifying 100 percent of all allowable business travel deductions. Just remember, you are required to keep all receipts for individual expenditures in excess of $75 per activity.

STRATEGY 63

Deduct 50 percent of your business entertainment expenses.

Deductible entertainment expenses must be both *ordinary* (common and accepted in your type of business) and *necessary* (helpful and appropriate, although not necessarily indispensable, to your business). Half (i.e., 50 percent) of the cost of business entertainment expenses is tax deductible, either as a directly related entertainment expense or as an associated entertainment expense.

1. *Directly related.* This includes entertainment that took place in a clear business setting or that was in the active conduct of business. Further, you must engage in business with the person during the entertainment period and have more than a general expectation that the activity will generate business income or some other specific business benefit.
2. *Associated.* This includes entertainment that is associated with your business and that either directly precedes or follows a substantial business discussion. This is generally interpreted to mean that the business discussion occurred within 24 hours prior to or after the event

---

STRATEGY 64

Deduct 50 percent of the cost of business-related meals.

Deduct business-related meals as business entertainment expenses. You are allowed to deduct 50 percent of your business meals that can reasonably be considered business entertainment in nature, subject to the following four guidelines:

1. You must discuss business before, during, or after a business meal.
2. The meal must have been arranged for the purpose of discussing specific business (not general, blue-sky, open discussions).
3. The meal must be in an environment where talking about business is possible.
4. You should properly document the entertainment business meal—with whom, where, and why.

STRATEGY 65

Deduct 50 percent of the cost of your season tickets.

You can deduct 50 percent of the cost of your season tickets if they are legitimate business expenses; however, you must take the deduction "by the event" and only for those specific events (games, concerts, etc.) that were deductible business expenses.

How you make the cost of these sporting and entertainment events tax deductible is based on tax law that allows the deduction if you discuss (legitimate) business topics at the event. The IRS realizes that sometimes that's impossible, so tax law has been amended to allow for the following modification. You are allowed to deduct 50 percent of the cost of the tickets if you either talk business at the event *or* you talk business with this very same individual or group of individuals 24 hours directly before or 24 hours directly after the event. This is referred to as the *associated rule*.

Keep in mind that business-related travel expenses are 100 percent tax deductible to your business, while entertainment and meals associated with business purposes are 50 percent tax deductible.

CHAPTER 14

Your Family and Yourself

As a small-business owner, you have an opportunity to hire your spouse, your children, and even your parents as a way of minimizing your family's tax burden. By shifting taxable business income to another family member, you can move dollars from higher tax rates to lower tax rates, thus creating real tax savings for you and your business.

Family Employee Benefits

STRATEGY 66

Hire your children to shift taxable dollars to them, tax-free up to $4850.

Pay your child for performing legitimate work for your business. For example, if your children are young (ages 5 through 12), you can pay them for performing the easier, less complicated, business tasks, such as emptying the business trash or washing the company car(s). If they are too young to perform these types of tasks, you can always include their picture in your business marketing brochure (if applicable). If they are older (say teenagers), you can give them more difficult tasks, such as filing and answering the phone.

Pay your children when they perform legitimate work in your business. Pay them contemporaneously (not just at year-end) and in the same manner as other employees—on a regular basis, by check. If you planned on giving them money anyway, this is a fantastic way to pay them wages that are tax deductible to your business and tax-free to them (up to the $4850 standard deduction), and you still get to claim your children as dependents on your personal income tax return. For wages in excess of $4850, the beginning tax rate is only 10 percent. If your form of business organization is unincorporated and you pay your children $400 or less, there's no self-employment or unemployment tax liability.

STRATEGY 67

Hire your parents to give them tax-deductible (before-tax) dollars from your business.

You can pay your parents wages (for legitimate work) with tax-deductible dollars from your business. These payments must be for legitimate work your parents do for your business.

The presumption is that you are already giving your parents money—perhaps to help them with their living expenses during their retirement. Since you're giving them money anyway from dollars that are left over after you've paid any and all taxes due, why not give them dollars that are tax deductible to your business? These tax-deductible (before-tax) dollars replace the (after-tax) dollars that you otherwise would have given them. In addition, because you are paying them with your business's before-tax (tax-deductible) dollars, there are more of these dollars to give them than would otherwise have been available (i.e., there would be fewer after-tax dollars than before-tax dollars by the amount of tax paid).

This allows your business to take a tax deduction for the wages you pay your parents; and even if your parents have to pay some tax on these wages, they may be in a lower tax bracket than either you or your business. In this manner, you may be shifting the tax burden from the higher tax rates applicable to your and your business to the lower tax rates enjoyed by your parents.

Owner Benefits

STRATEGY 68

Take advantage of tax-free owner benefits.

As a small-business owner, you are able to take advantage of tax-free owner benefits. These benefits are paid out of pretax dollars. This means that there are more of these dollars to spend, since no tax has been paid on these dollars. This allows you and your family to enjoy benefits that are paid by your business and that are also tax deductible to the business—the best of both worlds.

Here are some of the more important tax-free owner benefits that you can enjoy as a small business owner:

- *Adoption benefits.* Employer payments to a third party or reimbursements to an employee for qualified adoption expenses are generally tax-free up to a limit of $10,160 per adoption. The exclusion is phased out between $150,000 and $190,000 in income.
- *Athletic facilities.* The fair market value of athletic facilities, such as gyms, swimming pools, golf courses, and tennis courts, is tax-free if the facilities are on property owned or leased by the employer (not necessarily the main business premises) and used substantially by employees, their spouses, and dependent children. Such facilities must be open to all employees on a nondiscriminatory basis in order for the business to deduct related expenses.
- *Child or dependent care plans.* The value of day care services provided or reimbursed by an employer under a written, nondiscriminatory plan is tax-free up to a limit of $5000 per year ($2500 for married persons filing separately). Expenses are excludable if they would qualify for the dependent care credit. Employees must report employer-provided benefits on their individual tax returns to figure the tax-free exclusion. *Note:* Tax-free benefits reduce eligibility for the dependent care tax credit.
- *Tax credit for employer-provided child care expenses.* There is now a tax credit available to employers who provide child care for their employees. The credit equals the sum of 25 percent of the qualified child care expenditures, plus 10 percent of the qualified child care resource and referral expenditures. The maximum annual credit per employer is $150,000.
- *Minor fringe benefits.* These consist of small benefits that are administratively impractical to tax, such as occasional "supper money" (provided near the workplace) and taxi fares for overtime work, company parties, and occasional theater or sporting event tickets.
- *Discounts on company products and services.* Discounts on company products and services (that are usually sold to customers) provided to an employee are tax-free if the employer does not incur additional costs in providing them.
- *Education plans.* An exclusion of up to $5250 applies to employer-financed undergraduate courses (as of June 1, 2000).
- *Group term life insurance.* Premiums paid by employers are not taxed if policy cover-

age is $50,000 or less. The employee is taxed only on the cost of premiums for coverage in excess of $50,000.

- *Health insurance deduction for self-employed individuals.* Health insurance premiums are 100 percent deductible for self-employed individuals.
- *Health and accident coverage.* Employees are not taxed on contributions or insurance premiums made by the employer to health, hospitalization, or accident plans that cover employees, their spouses, or their dependents.
- *Long-term-care coverage.* An employee is not taxed on employer-provided long-term-care coverage that pays benefits in the event the employee becomes chronically ill.

Health Savings Accounts (HSAs)

STRATEGY 69

Establish and fund a Health Savings Account to make your health-related expenditures tax deductible.

Effective January 1, 2004, individuals (under age 65) may establish HSAs—custodial accounts allowing them to save for qualified medical and retiree health expenses on a tax-free basis. The individual, called an *account beneficiary,* must (for the months the HSA contributions are made) be covered under a high-deductible health plan (HDHP). Any eligible individual can establish an HSA. For HSA purposes, an "eligible individual" is (1) covered under a high-deductible health plan (HDHP) on the first day of such months, (2) *not* covered by any other health plan that is not an HDHP, (3) *not* entitled to benefits under Medicare, and (4) *not* claimed as a dependent on another person's tax return.

For self-only policies (i.e., a policy for yourself alone), a qualified health plan must have a minimum deductible of $1000, with a $5000 cap on out-of-pocket expenses. For family policies, a qualified health plan must have a minimum deductible of $2000, with a $10,000 cap on out-of-pocket expenses. These contributions are allowed up to 100 percent of the health plan deductible. The maximum annual HSA contribution for 2004 is $2600 for self-policies and $5150 for family policies. The monthly maximum contribution is equal to one-twelfth of the preceding, computed each month. Individuals from age 55 to 65 may make additional catch-up contributions of up to $500 in 2004 and increasing in $100 annual increments to $1000 annually in 2009 and thereafter.

Contributions made by individuals and family members are tax deductible for the account beneficiary—even if the account beneficiary does not itemize. Health Savings Account contributions are *not* on a use-or-lose basis—meaning that the account beneficiary does not lose his or her unused HSA dollars at the end of each year, such as was the case with the old Medical Savings Accounts (MSAs). Employer contributions are made on a pretax basis and are *not* taxable to the employee. Employers will be allowed to offer HSAs through a cafeteria plan; however, these employer contributions must be made available on a comparable basis (i.e., on behalf of all "participating employees").

Contributions must be made with a "qualified HSA" trustee or custodian—much in the same way that individuals establish IRAs. Your HSA trustee or custodian can be an insurance company, a bank, or a similar financial institution, as defined by the IRS. All existing already-approved IRA trustees or custodians are automatically approved as HSA trustees or custodians. *Note:* Your HSA does *not* have to be opened at the same institution that provides the HDHP. HSA distributions are tax-free if they are used to pay qualified medical expenses, which include the following:

- Amounts paid for the diagnosis, cure, mitigation, treatment or prevention of disease
- Prescription drugs
- Qualified long-term-care services and long-term-care insurance
- Continuation coverage required by federal law
- Health insurance for the unemployed
- Medicare expenses (but not Medigap)
- Retiree health expenses for individuals age 65 and older (*Note:* Retiree health plans would not have to meet the $1000 to $2000 minimum deductible requirements.)

Distributions made for any other purpose are subject to income tax and a 10 percent penalty. The 10 percent penalty is waived in case of death or disability. The 10 percent penalty is also waived for distributions made by individuals age 65 and older. In addition, upon death, HSA ownership may transfer to the spouse on a tax-free basis. *Note:* The payment of medically related expenses from your Health Savings Account is not subject to stringent IRS rules, therefore allowing you the discretion of what to include.

Working Condition Benefits

Benefits provided by an employer that would be deductible by an employee who paid the expenses him- or herself are tax-free working condition fringe benefits. Here are some applications:

- *Company cars.* The use of a company car is tax-free provided the car is used for business. If the car is used for personal use, the employee will be taxed on the value of such personal use.

    For many cars, the employer can use a flat mileage allowance (combined with an employee-maintained mileage log) to measure personal use.

    Regardless of personal use, an employee is not subject to tax for a company vehicle that the IRS considers to be of limited personal use (e.g., ambulance, flatbed truck, garbage truck, one-person truck, or refrigerated truck).

- *Company planes.* Use is tax-free to the extent it is used for business purposes.
- *Employer-paid business subscriptions.* Also included are reimbursed membership dues in professional associations.
- *Employer-provided education assistance.* Employer-paid undergraduate and graduate courses may be a tax-free working condition fringe benefit if the courses maintain or improve job skills but are not needed to meet your employer's minimum educational requirements and do not prepare the employee for a new profession.
- *Frequent flyer airline points.* This category also includes "frequent stayer" hotel points that employees accumulate personally for company-paid business trips.
- *Cafeteria plans.* Under a cafeteria plan, an employer can, in effect, increase an employee's take-home pay by paying, on behalf of each participating employee, benefit-related expenses with pretax dollars. Additionally, by reducing the employee's taxable income, the employer reduces its own liability for the matching portion of Social Security taxes, 7.65 percent of payroll, up to the maximum FICA wages threshold of $90,000. IRS regulations prohibit a sole proprietor, a partner (in a partnership), a member of an LLC (in most cases), or individuals who own more than 2 percent of an S corporation from participating in a cafeteria plan; however, such entities may still sponsor a plan and enjoy savings on payroll taxes attributable to other employees.

Flexible Benefit Plans

STRATEGY 70

Select the best application(s), for your business, from among the four major categories of flexible benefit plans available under the Section 125 cafeteria plans.

Following are the four major categories of flexible benefit plans under the Section 125 cafeteria plans, along with a description of the benefits covered under each major category:

1. *Premium-only plan (POP).* Under these plans, a portion of the employee's wages is redirected, on a pretax basis, to pay for a variety of employer-sponsored insurance premiums. These redirected wages are used to pay the employees' contributions toward health, life, dental, vision care, prescription drugs, and disability premiums. (*Note of caution:* If disability premiums are paid with pretax dollars, any disability payments received by the employee are taxable.)
2. *Flexible spending arrangements (FSA).* Flexible spending accounts redirect a portion of the employee's wages to pay for such benefits as health care, day care, and adoption expenses. During the year, employees are reimbursed from this account as they incur qualified expenses.
   The following restrictions apply to FSAs:

   - The election year must be made before the start of the year.
   - Employees elect the dollar amount of monthly installments to be withheld from their pay.
   - Once set up (new employees typically have 30 days in which to sign up), the employee may not discontinue, increase, or decrease coverage (unless there is a change in family or work status that falls under IRS guidelines or during the plan's one-time annual open enrollment period).
   - Only expenses incurred during the plan year may be reimbursed; however, an employer can pay an employee's expenses prior to the employee actually having enough in his or her account—provided the dollar amount paid is less than the employee's annual contribution.
   - A use-it-or lose-it rule applies: any unused balance at the end of the plan year is forfeited by the employee.
   - The types of expenses covered under an FSA include insurance deductibles and co-pays; vision care and glasses; prescription drugs; medical transportation; lab fees; laser eye surgery; hospital bills; oral surgery; X-rays; psychiatric care; dependent care, such as nanny expenses inside the home, dependent care outside the home, or day care registration fees for a child 12 years old or younger (up to $5,000 per year per employee, $2,500 if married filing separately); adoption expenses, up to $10,160 per year per adoption, for such expenses as court costs, attorney fees, and adoption fees. (*Note:* Long-term health care is not eligible.)

3. *Health reimbursement arrangements (HRA).* Health reimbursement arrangements allow an employer-funded account to repay the unreimbursed medical expenses of employees, with an option to carry unused funds forward.

   An HRA account may reimburse any or all the same expenses as an FSA (see item 2).

4. *Transportation benefit programs:* All participating employees are entitled to have a portion of their paycheck redirected to pay for transit passes (up to $100 per month), parking (up to $190 per month), and commuter highway vehicle expenses (up to $100 per month). Employees are reimbursed from this account as they incur transportation expenses.

Because you are the owner of your own business, you and your family are entitled to numerous tax benefits, allowing you to convert many of your personal expenditures into business tax deductions. For example, you can deduct child care, life insurance, and health insurance; and money formerly given to your children as allowances can now be paid to them as wages for working in your business, thus qualifying as a tax-deductible expense.

CHAPTER 15

Your Strategic Issues

As a small-business owner, you will find certain key issues become of concern from time to time; these are referred to as *strategic issues* because they require decisions that can be of strategic importance to your business. The topics of these issues vary and, for that reason, must be addressed separately, as they typically do not relate one to the other.

Net Operating Loss (NOL)

STRATEGY 71

Apply your business's net operating loss against your business's income.

As the owner of a business, you may from time to time incur either an actual loss or merely a tax loss created by the proper application of tax-saving strategies. In either case, the result is the same—your business will show a tax loss for the year in question. This is called a *net operating loss* (NOL). Depending on your form of business organization, this loss may be used to offset profits generated by other business entities that you own. If this is the case, this tax loss will have the effect of reducing your overall taxable income, thereby saving you considerable income tax liability.

If there is no current tax-year profit to offset, this net operating loss (NOL) can then be applied against (help reduce) the taxable income of other tax years, either (1) previously taxed income (prior years) and/or (2) future taxable income (future years).

If you elect to apply this net operating loss against the previously taxed income of prior year(s), this will reduce your business's income tax liability for the previous year(s) and could generate a tax refund right away for your business. If, on the other hand, you elect to apply the net operating loss against future years' taxable income, this will have the effect of reducing your business's taxable income for that future year. This will reduce your business taxable income for the year(s) in the future, and it may generate an even larger tax savings—depending on your business profit for the future year(s).

Staying Out of Trouble with the IRS

Staying out of trouble with the IRS means first that you understand all the critical tax requirements applicable to your business and second that you adhere to these requirements fully and on a timely basis. Discussions of some of the more important IRS requirements follow.

STRATEGY 72

File all payroll tax documents, and make all required payroll tax deposits.

Learn and use all applicable IRS procedures, forms, and filing and payment guidelines. As a business owner, you are required to prepare and file certain mandatory IRS tax forms, as well as numerous state and local government forms and documents. These may include the following forms and documents:

- *Federal Form SS-4.* This application requests information such as the type of business you are operating, your address, the form of business organization you have selected for your business, as well as other federally mandated information. When you complete this form and send it in, the IRS will issue a federal Employer Identification Number (EIN) for your business.
- *Form 941.* If you have employees, you are required to file this form with the IRS every quarter. This form summarizes the total amount of dollars your business withheld from your employees' pay, plus any employer matching portion that your business may be required to pay.

- *Federal income tax returns.* These are filed annually, after the end of the business's tax year, and might include a Schedule C, attached to your individual 1040 tax form (if your business is a sole proprietorship), Form 1065 (if your business is a partnership), Form 1102-S, or Form 1120-C (if your business is a corporation).
- *Fictitious name filings (with your state government).* This is a way to register and secure your business name.
- *State unemployment compensation forms.*
- *State workers' compensation forms.*

This is just a partial list of some of the documents and forms you are required to prepare and file. Although you can take care of these items yourself, I suggest that you hire a small-business accountant to do this work or, better yet, hire a payroll service to perform all payroll functions and all IRS-required payroll reporting functions, from quarterly payroll reports on through generating, distributing, and filing W-2s. Claim all documents issued to you when you prepare your individual income tax return.

STRATEGY 73

Avoid IRS audits by being aware of the IRS audit selection processes.

In truth, the chances of your business being audited are relatively slim. The actual number of businesses that are audited by the IRS is not public information; however, I'd be very surprised if the actual percentage of businesses that are ever audited exceeds 5 or 10 percent. Nevertheless, it's prudent for you as a business owner to be aware of the process the IRS uses to select tax returns for formal auditing. By understanding the process, you can take steps to minimize the chances of your business being audited.

The IRS selects its small-business audit targets in four ways:

1. *Random selection.* The IRS selects small businesses at random for audits.
2. *Targeted.* Certain types of small businesses are more apt to be audited (e.g., a sole proprietorship that loses money every year for a number of years).
3. *DIF scores.* The IRS is always on the lookout for extraordinary tax deductions in certain areas, particularly those that directly benefit only the owners, such as excess business travel, entertainment, company vehicles, and other owner-related perks. The IRS uses a relatively new method (as of 2002), Discriminate Index Function (DIF) ratios, to select returns for audit.

4. *Document compliance.* Anytime you fail to properly file your business tax return, it is at greater risk of an audit.

The best way for you to avoid having your business selected to be audited by the IRS is for you and your accountant to carefully apply the strategies contained within this book, *Make Your Life Tax Deductible*.

STRATEGY 74

**Avoid having business deductions disallowed by
documenting everything.**

If the IRS ever asks you for documentation supporting any tax deductions your business takes, the best way to comply with this request, and at the same time increase the chances for successfully justifying the business tax deductions in question, is for you to have full and accurate documentation for every tax deduction your business takes. The following tips are useful in complying:

- Keep your records for seven years to enable you to prove business tax deductions to which you are entitled.
- The burden of proof is on you, so be prepared to make your case.
- To the IRS, everything is taxable income and nothing is a deductible expense, *except* . . . as the IRS Code addresses the exceptions.
- Keep contemporaneous records as you go.
- Stay organized.
- Obtain and use a business credit card, or designate one or more personal card(s) exclusively for business use.

STRATEGY 75

**Carefully document and verify the status of independent contractors
when you hire them for your business.**

If you hire and pay as "independent contractors" those who are actually working as employees, your business may be liable for payroll taxes on these individuals. The IRS uses certain criteria to determine whether an individual is entitled to be paid as an independent contractor. Your business saves the cost of payroll taxes by hiring independent contractors (who are not entitled to payroll tax benefits) instead of wage-earning employees.

Apply the following IRS criteria to determine whether individuals are truly classified as independent contractors and can be hired as such:

- They hire, supervise, and pay their own employees.
- They are free to work when and for whom they wish.
- The work is done on their own premises.
- They are paid by the job or on a straight commission basis.
- They are subject to profit and loss.
- They may work for several businesses at one time.
- Their services are available to the general public.
- They can't be fired . . . except for breach of contract.

Note: You are required to prepare a 1099 (instead of a W-2) if you paid an independent contractor $600 or more for his or her services during any single tax year.

STRATEGY 76

Neither ignore nor automatically cave in and pay IRS tax deficiency notices, as the IRS is wrong much of the time.

Even though you may be tempted to assume that all correspondence you receive from the IRS is correct, take a good look to verify that the information contained in the notice is accurate. You never know the source of the inquiry, and even if you recognize the issue being presented by the IRS, there is certainly no assurance that the IRS's interpretation of the facts and its conclusions are always correct. You may be tempted, as many business owners are, to pay the deficiency in order to avoid the potential of further communication with, and further scrutiny from, the IRS; however, that may not be the best course of action.

For this reason, it's essential that you have a qualified CPA or an enrolled agent representing your business in any and all communications with the Internal Revenue Service (IRS).

STRATEGY 77

Make all required estimated tax deposits in full and on time.

Generally, you have to pay estimated tax payments if you expect to owe $1000 or more in taxes (including self-employment taxes) when you file your return. This means that you or your accountant will have to carefully monitor the profitability of your business throughout the tax year. If you are generating profits such that it is estimated that your business will have a substantial income tax liability at the end of the tax year (when your business income tax return is filed with the IRS), you are required to file (typically, quarterly) estimated income tax forms and to deposit the estimated income tax dollar deposits.

If you fail to file the proper form and do not pay the estimated taxes indicated to be due, your business may (and probably will) be assessed additional dollar penalties at the time your business's federal income tax return is filed. The likelihood and dollar amount of this additional penalty being assessed will depend on how much income tax your business actually winds up owing for the tax year in question.

STRATEGY 78

Select the proper tax year for your business.

As a small-business owner, you are obliged to select your business tax year from one of two options available to you:

1. *Calendar year.* Beginning January 1, and ending December 31. Once you adopt calendar, you must stay with it, unless you get IRS approval to change.
2. *Fiscal year.* Other than a calendar year; your business can operate (for tax purposes) during any 12 consecutive months, ending on the last day of any month except December. The one you select should take into consideration its impact on your business's income tax liability. There are some restrictions that limit your choice of tax year; however, for the most part you are well advised to select the tax year that is expected to minimize your business's income tax liability year after year.

You should select the tax year that best matches your business's taxable income and its tax-deductible expenses. In this manner, not only will you be able to see just exactly how much profit your business is generating, but there is also the greatest chance that your business's tax-deductible expenses will be able to offset your business's taxable income, thereby minimizing its income tax liability.

STRATEGY 79

Select the accounting method that minimizes your business's taxable income.

Account properly for all sales and purchases by selecting the proper accounting method (cash or accrual) that minimizes your business's potential (future) income tax liability.

- Under the *cash accounting method*, sales equal any cash received during the tax year, and expenses equal any cash expenditures during the same tax year. If you have no inventory and your credit sales (accounts receivable) are greater than your credit purchases (accounts payable), you are better served to select the cash basis of accounting.
- Under the *accrual accounting method*, sales equal any sales that were incurred during a given tax year (accounts receivable, whether collected or uncollected, during the same tax year); expenses equal any business expenses that were incurred during the same given tax year (accounts payable, whether paid or unpaid, during that same tax year). *Note:* If you have inventory, you are required to use the accrual basis of accounting. However, if you do not have inventory in your business and your credit sales (accounts receivable) are less than your credit purchases (accounts payable), you are better served to select the accrual basis of accounting. You *must* use the accrual method of accounting if your business has inventory (product for resale).

STRATEGY 80

Hire a great accountant (CPA or enrolled agent).

The importance of the accurate and complete reporting of your business's financial information cannot be overemphasized. Correctly creating and presenting the balance sheet, income statement, sources and uses of funds schedules, and cash flow analyses (to name a few of the most important) is critical to the financial success of your business. In a smaller business, the owner is often responsible for collecting financial information and passing it along to an outside accountant for review and statement preparation; in larger (but still considered "small") businesses, very often there is an internal accountant (an employee of the business) who works full-time on the business's financial matters and then submits financial information to an outside accountant.

The selection of this outside accountant is critical. This accountant should be someone who specializes in small-business accounting, *not* a general-purpose accountant who also has some business clients. Furthermore, you must ensure that your outside accountant is either a CPA or an enrolled agent. A *certified public accountant* (CPA) is a person who has passed a rigorous test to become certified to practice as a CPA in your state. Equally as appropriate for your small business is an *enrolled agent*, a person who is a practicing accountant and who has either worked for the Internal Revenue Service (as an employee) or passed a formal exam. The best choice for your business is either a CPA or an enrolled agent who is an ex-IRS employee . . . who is now on *your* side.

A number of strategic issues affect you as a business owner. These include, but are not limited to, the following: net operating loss (NOL), your relationship with the IRS (e.g., reporting requirements and the potential for IRS audits), record-keeping requirements, the use of independent contractors, your business's official tax year, and the importance of proper tax advice and counsel.

Your Retirement

Now you are two-thirds of the way to making your life tax deductible. All that remains is perhaps the most significant way business owners can not only further reduce their income tax liability, but at the same time begin the process of accumulating and growing their personal wealth: establishing and funding their own retirement plan—sponsored by their own business. "Your Retirement" is arguably the most powerful way you can accumulate substantial wealth, and do so on a tax-deferred basis or, in some cases, tax-free.

Part 3 includes the following chapters:

Although for most individuals retirement is inevitable, the financial quality of your retirement is not. It's up to you to ensure your retirement is funded at a dollar amount that will allow you the financial freedom you desire. When you work for someone else, the funding of your retirement nest egg is partially the responsibility of your employer; however, as the owner of a small business, it's your responsibility alone.

The Internal Revenue Service (IRS), under the guidance of the U.S. Congress, understands the need to assist and encourage small-business owners to create and fund their own retirement plans. Tax law applicable to small businesses includes a number of tax-based financial incentives to encourage small-business owners to take care of their own retirement and, in doing so, to take care of their employees as well.

The huge benefit of investing your business's tax-deductible dollars into your business's retirement plan is that, in addition to funding your retirement, you will most likely also create a significant amount of personal wealth. One of the major reasons you will be able to generate this wealth is the tax-favored treatment for contributions to a retirement plan. This is true whether you make your own contributions or your business makes them for you, so take advantage of the tremendous opportunities you have as a small-business owner to ensure your own wealth by creating and funding your own retirement plan(s).

Small-business owners can and must create and fund their business-based retirement plan(s). It's to this premise that Part 3 is dedicated. It's time to take the first step. . . .

STRATEGY 81

Fund your own tax-advantaged retirement plan and grow an enormous amount of personal wealth.

The purpose behind having your own personal retirement plan is to fund your retirement. Tax law allows you to do so in ways that are tax-advantaged. You may qualify to participate in certain retirement plans that are available to small-business owners, depending on factors such as your business's form of organization, other retirement plans in which you already participate, the amount of your earned income, and whether you are functioning as an employer (owner) or an employee of your business.

The key way to benefit is to invest early. The sooner you make contributions to your retirement plan(s), the greater the potential to accumulate more for your retirement. More dollars invested for a longer period of time translates into a greater number of dollars growing (tax deferred) at the rate of return that is generated by your retirement account(s). This creates a larger retirement nest egg for you! The dollars that you put into your retirement plan should be dollars that you don't need now and that you anticipate you can afford to leave in the plan until you retire.

Two tax-advantaged characteristics motivate small-business owners to arrange for the funding of their personal retirement plan(s):

1. Make contributions to your retirement plan using pretax dollars (i.e., earned income prior to paying any tax) that grow, tax deferred, until you retire. This allows you (1) to take a tax deduction for the tax year in which the contributions

were made and (2) to pay taxes on these contributed dollars, plus any growth in the value of the plan, when you retire. The presumption is that your tax rate when you retire will be lower than your current tax rate.

2. Make contributions to your retirement plan using after-tax dollars that grow, tax-free, forever. You do not get a tax deduction for the contributions you make; however, you never have to pay tax on either the contributed dollars or on any growth in the value of the plan.

Types of Retirement Plans

STRATEGY 82

Select the proper retirement plan for you and your business from IRA-based, defined contribution, and defined benefit plans.

The following sections discuss types of retirement plans that can be used by you and your business.

Traditional IRA

A traditional IRA is a retirement plan that allows individuals to make tax deductible contributions of $4000—to the extent of their earned income. This means that individuals may contribute the lesser of either income they have earned during a particular tax year or $4000. Contributions made into a traditional IRA are tax deductible to the individual in the year the contribution is made, and these contributions, and any growth in the value of the traditional IRA, are tax deferred until they are withdrawn at retirement.

Roth IRA

A Roth IRA is a retirement plan into which individuals are allowed to make contributions of $4000 to the extent of their earned income. This means the individual may contribute the lesser of income they have earned during a particular tax year, or $4000. Contributions made into a Roth IRA are made after tax (meaning they are not tax deductible when made). These contributions, and any growth in the value of the Roth IRA, are tax free forever.

SIMPLE IRA

A Savings Incentive Match Plan for Employees (SIMPLE) IRA was designed as an IRA plan especially for small businesses with 100 or fewer employees. It allows these businesses to offer a tax-advantaged, company-sponsored retirement plan to their employees.

A SIMPLE IRA is a salary-reduction retirement plan that qualifying small employers may offer to their employees. Salary-reduction contributions of up to $10,000 per year may be made by eligible employees, and their employers are required to make either matching contributions or a flat contribution.

SEP IRA

A simplified employee pension (SEP) IRA is a retirement plan that allows the employer to make contributions on behalf of each employee. The amount of annual contribution allowed per eligible employee is the lesser of (1) 25 percent of employee compensation up to $210,000 or (2) $42,000, up to the extent of each employee's compensation.

If you are self-employed, deductible contributions to your SEP IRA account may not exceed the lesser of (1) 20 percent of your net earnings up to $210,000 (after 50 percent of your net self-employment tax liability) or (2) $42,000, whichever is less.

Self-Employed 401(k), Individual 401(k), or Solo(k)

You should use this plan if you have no employees and don't expect to have any employees anytime soon. Two components comprise the maximum self-employed 401(k) plan contribution: an owner/employee salary-deferral contribution up to a maximum of $14,000 and an employer profit-sharing contribution up to a maximum of $42,000 (both contribution limits up to the extent of the owner/employee's earned income during the year in which the contribution is made)—or a combination of both (not to exceed a total of $42,000)—and all contributions are discretionary, which means you can elect to contribute or not.

Regular 401(k)

The regular 401(k) is designed for larger businesses, those with 20 or more employees. Contributions are made by the employee, using salary deferral, up to $14,000 annually, up to the extent of the employee's compensation; in addition, the employer can also make a contribution (on behalf of each eligible employee) of the lesser of $42,000 or 25 percent of the employee's compensation up to $210,000.

Keogh—Defined Contribution

The Keogh retirement plan was designed for self-employed individuals who function as both the employer and an employee; therefore, for purposes of a Keogh, the term *employee* includes a self-employed individual who has earned income. In other words, an owner/employee is both an employer and an employee.

The maximum contribution that can be made into a defined contribution Keogh retirement plan is the lesser of 100 percent of compensation up to $210,000, or $42,000. This total contribution can be made in one of three ways: (1) a profit-sharing contribution, plus (2) a money purchase contribution, the total of which, (1) plus (2), may not exceed the lesser of 100 percent of compensation up to $210,000, or $42,000 annually, or (3) a "paired" contribution, which is a combination of (1) and (2).

Solo-DB (Individual Defined Benefit)

A Solo-DB is a defined benefit retirement plan with a maximum annual contribution of $170,000. The Solo-DB plan is designed for business owners with no employees, unless the employees are partners in the business or spouses of the owners. With a Solo-DB plan you set a target dollar benefit that you want to receive when you retire. An actuary calculates your required annual contributions to the plan based on your target benefit, age, income, planned retirement age, and how much you have in the plan. These calculations are designed to create a plan that has an adequate amount of dollars in the plan (at the time of your retirement) sufficient enough to pay a specific (defined) benefit to you upon your retirement. Although the Solo-DB offers a tremendous opportunity to the account owner, it also lacks the flexibility of other plans.

Keogh—Defined Benefit

The Keogh defined benefit retirement plan was designed for self-employed individuals who function as both employer and employee; therefore, for purposes of a Keogh, the term *employee* includes a self-employed individual who has earned income. In other words, an owner/employee is both an employer and an employee.

The maximum contribution that can be made to a defined benefit Keogh retirement plan is determined actuarially to create a plan that has an amount of dollars in it (at the time of your retirement) sufficient enough to pay a specific (defined) benefit to you upon your retirement.

Earned Income

STRATEGY 83

Create the earned income (compensation) you need to qualify for participation in your personal retirement accounts.

You can qualify to participate in a retirement plan if you have earned income (compensation) for the tax year in question. The definition of earned income varies, depending on the form of organization your small business uses. Each form of business organization is listed here, along with the ways you can create earned income:

- For yourself and other owners
- For yourself as an employee of your business
- For your employees

Sole Proprietorship

1. For yourself as an owner: Your earned income is the bottom-line profit of the business.
2. For your employees: Wages you pay your employees.

One-Person Limited Liability Company (LLC-1)

1. For yourself as the member (owner): The bottom-line profit of the business is your earned income.
2. For your employees: Wages you pay your employees.

Partnership

1. For yourself as a working (partner) owner
   a. Your pro rata share of the partnership's bottom-line profit.

  b. "Guaranteed payments" you pay yourself (or other partners) for working in your partnership (even if the partnership doesn't make any profit). *Note:* Nonworking partners do not qualify for guaranteed payments.

 2. For your employees: Wages you pay your employees.

Limited Partnership

 1. For yourself as a working (partner) owner: "Guaranteed payments" you pay yourself (or other partners) for working in your limited partnership (even if the partnership doesn't make any profit).
 2. For your employees: Wages you pay your employees.

Limited Liability Company (LLC)

 1. For member-owners: Owners of an LLC are called *members.* If your form of business organization is a one-member LLC, you are the only member (owner). Because you are the only member, you are considered to be the *managing member* and therefore responsible for the day-to-day operations of the business. If your form of business organization is a multiple-member LLC, one member is the managing member, and the rest of the member-owners are members.

  The following are the sources of earned income for the managing member-owner and other member-owners alike:

  a. The member's pro rata share of the bottom-line profit of the LLC.
  b. Wages paid to member(s) for working in your LLC (even if the LLC doesn't make any profit).
  c. "Guaranteed payments" you pay yourself (or other members) for working in your LLC (even if the LLC doesn't make any profit). *Note:* Nonworking member-owners do not qualify for guaranteed payments.

 2. For your employees: Wages you pay your employees.

S Corporation

 1. For yourself as a working (shareholder) owner: Wages you pay yourself (or other shareholders) for working in your S corporation. *Note:* Nonworking shareholders do not qualify for wages.
 2. For your employees: Wages you pay your employees.

C Corporation

1. For yourself as a working (shareholder) owner: Wages you pay yourself (or other shareholders) for working in your C corporation. *Note:* Nonworking shareholders do not qualify for wages.
2. For your employees: Wages you pay your employees.

Contributions

STRATEGY 84

Make either tax-deferred or tax-free contributions to your own personal retirement plan account.

The annual tax-deductible or tax-deferred amount you are allowed to contribute to a retirement plan varies depending on the tax law applicable to that specific plan. Each plan is unique both in terms of what it is intended to accomplish and in the way tax law dictates that it will do so. The permissible dollar amounts of the contributions, as well as other limitations, are discussed in detail in Part 3, "Your Retirement."

Whichever type of contribution your retirement plan accommodates, you must make annual contributions into your personal retirement account, either on your own as a business owner (either tax deferred or tax-free), or through your business as a business tax deduction.

If you don't make annual contributions, you are missing out on two important aspects of retirement plan ownership: (1) You will miss out on the tax advantages of these contributions, and (2) you will not be able to accumulate tax-favored personal wealth from your own retirement plan account.

Your Investments

STRATEGY 85

Invest your retirement funds wisely.

After you decide on the type of retirement plan, you can consider the variety of investment options. One decision you will need to make in designing a plan is whether to permit your employees to direct the investment of their own accounts or whether you should manage the monies on their behalf. If you choose the former, you also need to decide which investment options to make available to the participants. Depending on the plan design you choose, you may want to hire someone to determine the investment options to make available and/or to manage the plan's investments. Continually monitoring the investment options ensures that your selections remain in the best interests of your plan and its participants.

Retirement account investments include the following types of accounts: banks, credit unions, certificates of deposit (CDs), mutual funds, and certain limited partnerships (to name a few). The accounts are technically *trust* or *custodial* accounts that are managed by an account trustee and are purposely out of the day-to-day reach of the retirement account owner.

If you have a *self-directed* retirement plan account, you can direct the plan's trustee to invest your retirement dollars in a broader array of options, including real estate investments.

Distribution Methods

STRATEGY 86

Select the appropriate distribution method for your retirement plan, depending on your age and circumstances.

Payments you receive from your non-Roth IRA retirement funds are taxed at your regular income tax rates upon withdrawal, and they are added to your total yearly income, then taxed at your marginal income tax rates (the rates that apply to the next dollar you earn). One of the factors that you may consider when establishing the timing of distributions from your retirement account(s) is the potential for taking your distributions during years in which you have greater deductions, such as during years of increased charity giving or in years you incur tax losses from selling your non-retirement-plan-related securities investments. Correctly matching these two events can considerably reduce the tax rate applicable to your retirement plan distributions. This occurs because your tax losses reduce the dollar amount of taxable income on which you must pay income taxes for a given tax year, and therefore you may find yourself in a lower marginal tax rate for that year.

Distributions are taxed depending on both your age at the time you take the distribution and the total dollar amounts that you distribute to yourself during each tax year. If you don't wish to take the entire balance out of your retirement account, you are allowed to take partial distributions.

Under Age 59½

STRATEGY 87

Use the following distribution options if you are under age 59½.

The tax laws applicable to retirement plans are not designed to encourage distributions prior to the time the account owner reaches age 59½. For example, tax law imposes an additional 10 percent tax penalty (in addition to the account owner's applicable personal income tax rate) on any dollars that are distributed prior to age 59½—unless the distributions fall under very specific exceptions to the tax penalty. Tax law doesn't encourage these early distributions; however, if the circumstances are within the exceptions, the 10 percent tax penalty is waived. Furthermore, if the retirement account owner has a pressing need, he or she can pay the 10 percent tax penalty on any dollars withdrawn, plus the income tax due, and use these dollars as he or she sees fit.

The following are the methods of taking distributions that are allowed if you are under age 59½.

All Retirement Plans

1. You may take distributions as part of a "series of substantially equal periodic payments" over the life expectancy of the owner of the retirement account, or the life expectancies of the owner and the beneficiary, using one of the following annuity-type methods:

    a. Type 1. An annuity purchased by the employer providing annual payments to the employee during the employee's expected retirement (actuarially determined).

    b. Type 2. The "fixed amortization method," whereby you amortize your retirement account balance like a mortgage, using life expectancy tables. Any interest rate that is reasonable may be used; however, the preferred rate is 120 percent of the federal midterm rate for either of the two months immediately preceding the month in which the distribution begins.

    c. Type 3. The "fixed annuitization method," similar to type 2 except that it uses a mortality table as the basis for the annual distribution allowed.

2. If you do a rollover into another retirement account, use a trustee-to-trustee transfer. If you take a distribution, the following applies:

    a. A 20 percent backup income tax withholding will be deducted (and sent in to the IRS) from the proceeds, and you are required to make up the shortfall created by this 20 percent backup withholding prior to completing the rollover.

    b. If you fail to roll over these dollars into another retirement plan within 60 days, you will incur a 10 percent tax penalty, plus any income tax due.

3. You are allowed to take a distribution up to the dollar amount of medical expenses that are more than 7.5 percent of your adjusted gross income (AGI), and you do not have to itemize to meet this exception.

4. You may take distributions if you receive unemployment payments for 12 consecutive weeks, and when you pay health insurance premiums, you are allowed to take distributions up to the dollar amount of these health insurance premiums.

5. You may take distributions if you are totally and permanently disabled.

IRA-Based Retirement Plans

STRATEGY 88

Use the following distribution options if you are under age 59½ and have an IRA-based retirement plan.

1. Take distributions as part of a "series of substantially equal periodic payments" over the life expectancy of the owner, or life expectancies of the owner and the beneficiary, under the following conditions if your retirement plan is an IRA-based plan (traditional IRA, SIMPLE IRA, or SEP IRA):

    a. Begin at any age, based on a lifetime payout calculation.

b. Account owner can still be employed.

c. The "series of substantially equal periodic payments" must continue for a minimum of five (5) years, or until the account owner becomes age 59½.

2. Take distributions equal to or less than your qualified higher-education expenses. These distributions are for IRA-based retirement plans only: If you pay qualified higher-education expenses for yourself, your spouse, your children, or your grandchildren, you are allowed to take distributions up to the dollar amount of these higher-education expenses.

3. Take distributions to pay for your first-time home purchase, up to $10,000. If you are buying, building, or rebuilding a principal residence, you may take distributions equal to the dollar amount of these expenses, up to a lifetime maximum of $10,000, under the first-time home purchase exception, provided you have not owned a principal residence during the past two years. Qualified expenses include acquisition costs, settlement charges, and closing costs. You have 120 days from the date of distribution within which to complete the work. This applies to traditional and Roth IRAs only. If you are under the age of 59½, you cannot withdraw funds from your 401(k) plan to purchase your first home without being subject to a 10 percent additional tax on early distributions from qualified retirement plans. However, depending on the rules for your 401(k) plan, you may be able to borrow money from your 401(k) plan to purchase your first home. Your plan administrator should have written information about your particular plan that explains when you can borrow funds from your 401(k) plan and any other plan rules.

4. Take distributions to pay health insurance premiums if you are unemployed and receive unemployment payments for 12 consecutive weeks. Under such circumstances, you are allowed to take distributions up to the dollar amount of these health insurance premiums.

Qualified Retirement Plans Other Than IRA-based

STRATEGY 89

Use the following distribution options if you are under age 59½ and have a qualified retirement plan other than an IRA-based retirement plan.

Distributions are allowed, out of either a defined contribution or a defined benefit retirement plan, as part of a series of substantially equal periodic payments over the life expectancy of the owner, or life expectancies of the owner and the beneficiary, under the following conditions:

1. If you left the company during or after the calendar year in which you reached age 55.
2. If you, as the account owner, have incurred "separation of service" from your employer (you have left the company).
3. If the "series of substantially equal periodic payments" continues for a minimum of five years, or until the account owner becomes age 59½. The dollar amount of these distributions are subject to the following maximum distribution limitations:

   a. *If a defined contribution retirement plan.* The annual addition to a participant's account may not exceed the lesser of 100 percent of the participant's compensation (not exceeding $210,000) or $42,000.

   b. *If a defined benefit retirement plan.* May not exceed the lesser of $170,000 or 100 percent of the participant's average compensation (not exceeding $210,000) for the participant's three consecutive years of highest compensation.

Age 59½ and Older

STRATEGY 90

Use the following distribution options if you are age 59½ and older.

During this time period, you have considerable discretion in determining the dollar amount of distributions that you will take. There are no applicable minimum distributions, and the only other restrictions are those imposed by the maximum distribution limitations applicable to both defined contribution and defined benefit employer-sponsored retirement plans.

Allowed Distribution Methods

If you made tax-deductible (tax-deferred) contributions into any retirement plan, you are allowed to make distributions to yourself using either of the following methods. However you are not required to take any money out of your retirement account(s).

1. *The "any dollar amount at any time" method.* Remember, you must pay any income taxes due.
2. *The "lump-sum" method.* This requires a distribution of the account owner's entire account balance. The balance must be distributed (received) within a single tax year, and account owners are liable for income taxes at their own ordinary marginal income tax rate. For 10-year averaging, the tax is calculated using what the tax rates would have been if the lump sum received had been spread out over a 10-year period.

    Account owners born before January 2, 1936, have two options within the lump-sum method:

    a. **Option 1.** Use 10-year averaging. Under this method, the ordinary income tax due is calculated using what tax rates would have been applicable if the lump sum received had been spread out over a 10-year period. The purpose of this is to reduce the income tax liability of the account owner upon receiving a lump-sum distribution. The presumption is that the average tax rate (over 10 years) would be lower than the account owner's marginal tax rate if it were applicable to the entire lump-sum distribution received.

    b. **Option 2.** Pay a separate 20 percent tax on the pre-1974 portion, plus 10-year averaging on the balance.

If you made non-tax-deductible (after-tax) contributions to any retirement plan, you are allowed distributions to yourself in any amount, at any time, and you owe no income taxes on these distributions. *Note:* You would already have paid income taxes due on your contributed dollars at the time you made these non-tax-deductible (after-tax) contributions.

Required Minimum Distribution (RMD)

If the sum-total balance of all the account owner's retirement accounts has not been distributed by the account owner's 70½ birthday, the following optional distribution methods apply:

1. If you're still working and you have an employer-sponsored retirement plan (such as a defined contribution or a defined benefit plan), you may wait until you actually retire before you must take required minimum distributions (RMDs). If you own a retirement plan (excluding a Roth IRA), you must start taking required minimum distributions as soon as you reach age 70½.
2. If you're not still working, you must take required minimum distributions as soon as you reach age 70½. When the retirement account owner reaches age 70½, he or

she is required to take at least a minimum dollar amount of total distributions from all retirement account(s) combined. The retirement account owner must calculate a certain minimum distribution amount for each year after age 70½.

STRATEGY 91

Be aware that you may be required to start taking required minimum distributions from your retirement account(s) when you reach age 70½.

You must start to withdraw dollars from the account in the year you reach 70½ (except for a Roth IRA, for which there are no mandatory distribution requirements). If you do not, a penalty of 50 percent applies to the difference between the minimum amount you should have received and the amount you did receive. Keep in mind, however, that you cannot make contributions after you have reached age 70½.

When withdrawals are made each year after attaining 70½, they are made based on IRS life expectancy tables. The intent of the law is that your retirement account be zeroed out on the day you die. All distributions are fully taxable, except for amounts allocable to nondeductible contributions, such as in the instance of a Roth IRA.

If you continue to work past age 70½ and you own less than 5 percent of the business, you can put off withdrawals past age 70½. However, if you own 5 percent or more of the business and you don't work past age 70½, you must start withdrawing funds by age 70½.

Therefore, when you reach the age of 70½, you must begin to take the required minimum distributions (RMDs) from your retirement plan (except for a Roth IRA, for which there are no mandatory distribution requirements). Calculating the RMD for each retirement account used to be a rather complicated and time-consuming process; however, new tax law has made this process much easier. The new tax law also allows you to withdraw less—if you wish. This is particularly useful to new retirees who have enough income from other sources and who want to withdraw (as a distribution) as little as possible from their IRAs and let the accounts grow in value for a longer period of time.

STRATEGY 92

Calculate your minimum required distribution annually.

The required annual minimum distributions can be calculated by dividing an account's year-end value by the distribution period determined by the IRS. Table P3.1, the Uniform Lifetime Table, is the most commonly used of three life-expectancy charts that help retirement account holders calculate mandatory distributions. (The other two tables are used for beneficiaries of retirement funds and account holders who have much younger spouses.)

The IRS wants to collect tax on your individual retirement account balances before you die. It wants its money before you leave your money to your heirs, so you are forced to distribute a portion of your retirement funds each year after you turn 70½.

When you turn 70½, you have until April 1 of the following year to take at least the required minimum distribution out of your retirement accounts. This RMD must come out of retirement accounts for which taxes have been deferred. This applies to the traditional IRA, the SIMPLE IRA, the SEP IRA, and certain employer-sponsored plans.

Table P3.1   Uniform Lifetime Table for Required Minimum Distributions (RMDs)

To calculate the year's minimum distribution amount, take the age of the retiree and find the corresponding distribution period. Then divide the value of your retirement account by the distribution period to find the required minimum distribution.

Age of Retiree	Distribution Period (in years)	Age of Retiree	Distribution Period (in years)	Age of Retire	Distribution Period (in years)
70	27.4	86	14.1	102	5.5
71	26.5	87	13.4	103	5.2
72	25.6	88	12.7	104	4.9
73	24.7	89	12.0	105	4.5
74	23.8	90	11.4	106	4.2
75	22.9	91	10.8	107	3.9
76	22.0	92	10.2	108	3.7
77	21.2	93	9.6	109	3.4
78	20.3	94	9.1	110	3.1
79	19.5	95	8.6	111	2.9
80	18.7	96	8.1	112	2.6
81	17.9	97	7.6	113	2.4
82	17.1	98	7.1	114	2.1
83	16.3	99	6.7	115 or older	1.9
84	15.5	100	6.3		
85	14.8	101	5.9		

Note: The Roth IRA is exempt from these RMD rules because Roth IRAs do not have balances for which taxes have been deferred.

If you fail to make the required minimum distribution, the IRS will levy the 50 percent excess accumulation tax on the required distribution that you didn't take. If you can convince the IRS that your distribution shortfall was a reasonable error and you're taking steps to rectify the situation, the IRS could waive the excess-accumulation tax penalty. You can always take more dollars out of your retirement account; however, that won't affect required minimum distributions for future years.

If you have multiple retirement accounts, you must figure the annual minimum required distribution amount for each account. Fortunately, you don't have to take distributions out of each retirement account; rather you can add up the separate account balances and then take the total due from just one account.

The IRS will let you take your required distribution in installments; just make sure that these installment disbursements (monthly, quarterly, etc.) total at least the yearly minimum amount you're obligated to withdraw. Be aware that these required minimum distributions cannot be converted into a Roth IRA.

Self-Directed Retirement Accounts

STRATEGY 93

Take control of your retirement account investments by converting your IRA-based retirement plan into a self-directed retirement plan.

If you wish to take a more active role in managing your retirement account investments, you may set up a self-directed retirement plan. If your retirement account is self-directed, you are allowed to decide, within the existing IRS guidelines, how, when, and where your retirement monies will be invested. For example, rather than investing your retirement monies in a mutual fund, where the fund manager decides when and where to invest (taking your overall guidelines into consideration), you decide specifically where your monies are to be invested when you own a self-directed retirement plan. This allows you, for example, to invest your retirement monies in real estate investments (e.g., buying and selling residential and/or commercial properties).

If your retirement plan is IRA-based (traditional IRA, Roth IRA, SIMPLE IRA, or SEP IRA), you can move your account balances from your non-self-directed retirement account(s) into new self-directed retirement account(s). The preferred way to move these monies is to order a trustee-to-trustee transfer directly from your old retirement account (trustee) to your new retirement account (trustee). This trustee-to-trustee transfer avoids the potential for any penalties and income tax due if you take possession of your retirement account dollars and fail to properly and in a timely way move these monies into your new self-directed accounts.

Compound Interest

STRATEGY 94

Take advantage of the power of compound interest in retirement plan account growth.

Your money is able to compound much faster, without the eroding factor of taxes, through the power of compound interest in either a tax-deferred or a tax-free retirement account. With a traditional or Roth IRA, you are allowed to contribute only $4000; however, it is possible for you to contribute much more annually to a retirement account of your own sponsored by your business. By contributing these additional dollars to your retirement account(s), by taking advantage of the power of compound interest and the ability for these retirement dollars to grow either tax deferred or tax-free, you will be able to grow your wealth just that much faster.

Wearing Two Hats

STRATEGY 95

Understand how you may wear two hats—as a business owner and an employee of the business.

Contributions made by either the employer-owner or the employee of a business go directly into the retirement account owner's retirement account(s). As the owner of your own business, you have the benefit of contributing to your own retirement account(s), as the *owner* of your business (when the business makes a profit) and/or as the *employee* of your business (by receiving wages from your business and/or guaranteed payments, even when your business doesn't generate any profit).

Being able to add contributions to your personal retirement account from two distinct sources is a very powerful special opportunity that most business owners have, depending on your business's form of business organization. For example, a sole proprietor is not allowed to pay him- or herself wages, so the owner is limited to making contributions to a retirement plan based strictly on the bottom-line profit of the business. This means that the owner is not allowed to generate earned income from either wages or guaranteed payments, and therefore the business must be profitable for the business owner to qualify to make a retirement plan contribution for the tax year in question.

Business Eligibility

STRATEGY 96

Make your business eligible to provide a business-based retirement plan for you and your employees.

Depending on the type of retirement plan and the type of business, different eligibility requirements must be met. The details of business eligibility are discussed for each respective plan in Chapters 16 to 22. Your business is required to have certain very specific characteristics in order to meet the eligibility requirements of a given retirement plan.

Employee Eligibility

STRATEGY 97

Qualify your employees to be participants in a retirement plan sponsored by your business.

Depending on the type of retirement plan, different requirements must be met in order for the employees to be eligible to participate in the business's chosen retirement plan. The details of employee eligibility are discussed for each respective plan in the applicable chapters in this book.

Employee eligibility requirements are critical to your business's ability to provide a specific retirement plan for its employees. Failure to meet the minimum employee eligibility requirements will mean that your business may not implement that specific retirement plan.

As an owner-employee of your business, it's important that you understand the dual functions of the term *employee*, which, for purposes of retirement plans, includes self-employed individuals who have earned income from W-2 wages received as an employee of their own business or, if the business generates profit, for the tax year in question. As an owner-employee of your own business, you are both an employer and an employee.

Tax-Free Rollovers

STRATEGY 98

Use a trustee-to-trustee transfer to move retirement account funds from one retirement account to another.

When you transfer account funds from one retirement account to another, you must be careful how you move these funds. The best way to move funds is to initiate a direct transfer, called a *trustee-to-trustee transfer*. Using a direct transfer, you instruct the trustee of your new retirement account to contact the trustee of your old retirement account to request that all or part of your retirement funds be sent by the old trustee to the new trustee. In this manner, you are completely removed from the process and do not take part in the actual transfer of the funds. If you were to take possession of the funds personally, handing them off to your new trustee, you would be subject to certain IRS rules that charge a penalty if these funds are not handled properly and in a timely manner. For example, if you take funds out of one of your retirement accounts as a rollover, and don't place them in your new retirement account within 60 days, you are subject to a 10 percent penalty, plus any tax due on the dollars you took out and didn't replace in time.

A tax-free rollover may occur only once in a one-year period, starting on the date you receive the first distribution, and this rule applies separately to each of your retirement accounts. Trustee-to-trustee transfers are not taxable events, because you do not receive the funds. The law does not require a waiting period between transfers, whereas rollovers are subject to a once-a-year limitation.

STRATEGY 99

Never purchase tax-free investments for your retirement accounts.

It makes absolutely no sense for you to use tax-free investments to fund your retirement account. Your retirement account is already tax-favored, so the tax-free status of these investments would be wasted. Furthermore, the rate of return (yield) on tax-free investments is generally much lower than on comparable investments that are taxable, and you are certainly interested in maximizing the rate of return on your investments.

Retirement can sneak up on you and your family. The best way to prepare is to start making tax-favored contributions to your business-sponsored retirement plan as soon as possible.

CHAPTER 16

Individual Retirement Accounts (IRAs)

Types of IRA-Based Retirement Plans

STRATEGY 100

Select your IRA-based retirement plan from the following
four retirement plans.

Four types of retirement plans use an IRA as the cornerstone of the plan: traditional IRAs, Roth IRAs, SIMPLE IRAs, and SEP IRAs.

Although each plan differs in both its structure and intent, the common component in each is that the individual account owners have each either established and funded their own IRA or, in some instances, been assisted in doing so by their employer.

Both a traditional IRA and a Roth IRA are similar in that they are retirement plans that allow individuals to make tax-deductible contributions of $4000 per year, to the extent of their earned income. The differences relate to how both the annual contributions and distributions (made at the time of the IRA owner's retirement) are taxed. Contributions to a traditional IRA are tax deductible to the owner of the plan, and these contributions, plus any growth in the value of the IRA, are tax deferred. This means that no tax is due until distributions are made to the IRA owner at the time of his or her retirement. Under a Roth IRA, annual contributions are not tax deductible when they are made; however, all contributions, plus any growth in the value of the IRA, are tax-free. This means that when distributions are made, no tax is due on either the contributions or the increase in value.

A SIMPLE IRA is a salary-reduction retirement plan that qualifying small employers may offer to their employees. Salary-reduction contributions of up to $10,000 per year may be made by eligible employees, and their employers are required to make either matching contributions or a flat contribution.

A SEP IRA is a retirement plan that allows the employer to make contributions on behalf of each employee, and employees can also make separate contributions to their own SEP IRA retirement account. The amount of annual contribution allowed per eligible employee is the lesser of 25 percent of (1) employee compensation up to $210,000, or (2) $42,000, up to the extent of each employee's compensation. All contributions are made by the employer—no employee contributions are allowed.

STRATEGY 101

Net your self-employment profit from your multiple businesses in determining your eligibility for IRA contributions.

If you are self-employed, and if you have multiple businesses, you must net the profit from them against any losses your businesses may show in determining whether or not you have the earned income required to qualify for making contributions into your retirement account(s) for the current tax year. Even if one of your businesses makes a profit, you haven't yet met the earned income requirement necessary for retirement plan contributions if you have one or more businesses that generate losses. You are required to net any and all business losses against any business profits. If this is a positive (earned income) value, you are allowed to make retirement contributions up to the lesser of either your net earned income or the maximum contribution limits for your retirement account type.

Spousal and Children IRAs

STRATEGY 102

Take advantage of the spousal and child IRA rules to include the rest of your family in your business's retirement plan.

The spousal IRA allows a married person to make a self-directed IRA contribution for his or her spouse. A couple can contribute up to 100 percent of their combined earned incomes or $8000, whichever is less (plus an extra $500 per person under the catchup provision if both individuals are age 50+, bringing the total to $9000).

If your spouse has income, or you file jointly, do not forget about having your spouse open a self-directed traditional or Roth IRA. In addition, your spouse is eligible to open a SEP, SIMPLE, or self-employment 401(k) IRA if he or she has income from your business.

Tax law allows up to a $4000 ($4500 for individuals age 50 or older) spousal (non-working) IRA contribution in addition to your $4000 ($4500 for individuals age 50 or older) regular IRA contribution, as long as your combined earned income and wages cover both contributions.

Remember, your children can also have an IRA if they have earned income (compensation from your business). You may create an IRA for your children based on income they earn for performing legitimate work for your business. And your children can use the accumulated balance in their traditional IRA to purchase their first home—up to $10,000.

Non-Tax-Deductible Contributions

STRATEGY 103

Make non-tax-deductible contributions to your retirement plan if you don't qualify for tax-deductible contributions.

You are allowed to make non-tax-deductible contributions into your retirement account(s) up to the maximum contribution amounts allowed by tax law. This means that if for some reason you do not qualify to make tax-deductible contributions, you can still make after-tax (non-tax-deductible) contributions for a given tax year. The advantage of making these non-tax-deductible contributions is that even though you won't get a current-year tax deduction for your contributions, you do enjoy the benefit of your money growing tax deferred until you retire. Just remember that the best approach is to maximize your tax-deductible contributions first, then consider making nondeductible contributions up to the allowed contributions limits.

Furthermore, these nondeductible contributions can be withdrawn tax-free at any time, and any growth in the value of your retirement account is taxed at the time of withdrawal (except in the case of a Roth IRA, which grows tax-free forever).

Borrow to Contribute

STRATEGY 104

If you're short on cash, borrow to contribute to your retirement plan account.

Make your tax-deductible IRA contribution even if you're short on cash—by borrowing the money. If an IRA deduction entitles you to a refund, you can file the return early, claim the IRA deduction, and, if you receive the refund in time, apply it toward an IRA contribution before the due date. If you don't get your refund in time, plan to borrow the money (paying the small amount of interest due on the short-term loan) to pay the deducted IRA contribution, then repay the loan when you receive your tax refund.

Four IRA-based retirement plans are available to you as a business owner: (1) traditional IRA, (2) Roth IRA, (3) SIMPLE IRA, and (4) SEP IRA. Each of these offers a unique opportunity for you to set aside tax-favored dollars for your retirement.

CHAPTER 17

Traditional IRA

STRATEGY 105

Set up and fund a traditional IRA when you want to contribute a small amount of before-tax dollars to a retirement plan and let your money grow tax deferred until you retire.

A traditional IRA is a retirement plan that allows individuals to make tax-deductible contributions of $4000, to the extent of their earned income. This means that individuals may contribute the lesser of income they have earned during a particular tax year, or $4000. Contributions made to a traditional IRA are tax deductible to the individual in the year the contribution is made. These contributions, and any growth in the value of the traditional IRA, are tax deferred until they are withdrawn at retirement in the form of a distribution to the account owner.

Traditional IRAs for the taxable year can be opened and/or funded anytime prior to the due date for your individual Form 1040 tax return, excluding extensions. This means anytime prior to April 15 of the calendar year following the tax year in which the deduction is being considered. This due date is applicable to both deductible and nondeductible Roth IRA contributions. Remember, filing for an extension of time does not mean you can extend the time period for contributions.

You must make your contributions to your traditional IRA as an individual taxpayer, and you may set up your traditional IRA in any one of the following three ways:

1. Make annual tax-deductible contributions. Each tax year you are allowed to make a tax-deductible contribution to your Traditional IRA.
2. Make annual non-tax-deductible contributions into your traditional IRA.
3. At any time, you are allowed to roll over account balances from an employer plan or from another IRA into your traditional IRA.

Earned Income

You can qualify to participate in a retirement plan if you have earned income (compensation) for the tax year in question under the following conditions:

- If you earned profits in your business
- If you paid yourself wages as an employee of your business
- If you paid yourself "guaranteed payments"—even if your business earned no profits

You are allowed to contribute to your retirement plan the dollar amount of your earned income for the tax year in question, up to the maximum allowed contribution limit for the type of retirement plan you own.

Contributions

STRATEGY 106

Contribute to your traditional IRA up to a maximum of $4000 annually.

An *individual retirement account* (IRA) is an account that allows you to contribute annually the lesser of $4000 ($4500 for individuals age 50 or older) or 100 percent of your earned income per year—if neither you nor your spouse is an active participant in an employer or self-employed retirement plan. If you have coverage, you may claim a deduction if your adjusted gross income is below a specified phaseout range, and you're not allowed to make contributions past age 70½.

Modified AGI Limits

STRATEGY 107

Keep an eye on the modified adjusted gross income (MAGI) restrictions when you're making contributions into your traditional IRA.

You are prohibited from contributing for any year in which you generated too much modified adjusted gross income (MAGI) during that year, subject to the MAGI limits applicable to a traditional IRA is discussed subsequently.

Phaseout thresholds are based on your modified adjusted gross income (generally the total income shown on your tax return plus or minus adjustments to income, other than IRA contributions).

You are considered an active participant in an employer retirement plan if you are covered by a retirement plan. In this instance, you are considered "covered" if contributions are allowed to be made or allocated to your account for the plan year that ends within your tax year—even if no contributions are made by you or your employer into your account for the tax year in question.

If you are an active participant in a retirement plan, or if you are considered to be an active participant because of your spouse's participation, the $4000 IRA deduction limit ($4500 for individuals age 50 or older) is phased out when your modified adjusted gross income (AGI) exceeds a phaseout threshold. Table 17.1 shows the dollar amount at which the phaseout begins depending on your marital status.

Table 17.2 shows the ranges within which your traditional IRA tax-deductible contribution is phased out.

Distributions

The methods available for you to take distributions out of your traditional IRA depend on your age and other circumstances. This section examines each different circumstance.

Table 17.1   AGI Phaseout Thresholds

$50,000 If you are single, head of household, or married filing separately and treated as single because you lived apart from your spouse.

$70,000 If you are married filing jointly and both you and your spouse were active plan participants, or you are a qualifying widow or widower.

$70,000 If you are married filing jointly and you are an active plan participant, but your spouse was not. You use the $70,000 threshold, and your spouse also uses the same $150,000 threshold.

$150,000 If you are married filing jointly and you are not an active plan participant, but your spouse was; you use the $150,000 threshold, and your spouse uses the $54,000 threshold.

$0 If you are married filing separately and lived with your spouse at any time during the tax year, and either you or your spouse actively participated in the plan during the tax year, both you and your spouse are subject to the $0 threshold as long as you lived together at any time during the tax year and either was an active plan participant during the tax year.

Under Age 59½

You can take distributions out of your traditional IRA retirement plan if you are under age 59½ using the following methods.

1. You may take distributions as part of a "series of substantially equal periodic payments" over the life expectancy of the retirement account owner, or life expectancies of the owner and the beneficiary, using one of the following annuity-type methods:
   a. An annuity purchased by your employer
   b. The fixed amortization method
   c. The fixed annuitization method

   Under the series of substantially equal periodic payments method, the following apply:

Table 17.2   Phaseout Range for the $4000 Tax Deduction ($4500 for individuals age 50 or older)

If Your Phaseout Threshold Is:	Deduction Limit Is Phased Out If MAGI Is	No Deduction If MAGI Is:
$50,000	$50,001–$59,999	$60,000 or more
$70,000	$70,001–$79,999	$80,000 or more
$150,000	$150,001–$160,999	$160,000 or more
$0	$0–$9,999	$10,000 or more

    a. You may begin at any age, based on a lifetime payout calculation.
    b. Account owner can still be employed.
    c. The series of substantially equal periodic payments must continue for a minimum of five (5) years, or until the account owner becomes age 59½.

2. You may do a rollover into another retirement account.
3. You may pay medical expenses in excess of 7.5 percent of your adjusted gross income (AGI).
4. You may pay your health insurance if you are unemployed.
5. You may take distributions if you are permanently disabled.
6. You may take distributions for your higher-education expenses.
7. You may take distributions to pay for your first-time home purchases, up to $10,000.

Age 59½ and Older

During this time period, you have considerable discretion in determining the dollar amount of distributions that you will take. If you made tax-deductible (tax-deferred) contributions to your retirement plan, you can take distributions in either of two ways:

1. The "any dollar amount at any time" method: Take out any dollar amount you wish, whenever you want.
2. The "lump-sum" method: Take out the entire balance in your retirement account all at once.

Either way, you are required to pay any and all income tax due on the dollar amount of any distributions you receive in any given tax year unless 10-year averaging applies to the lump sum. However, if you made nondeductible (after-tax) contributions to your retirement plan, you can take distributions in any amount, at any time, and you would owe no income taxes on these distributions.

Required Minimum Distribution (RMD)

If the total balance of all the account holder's retirement accounts has not been distributed by the account holder's 70½ birthday, the following optional distribution methods apply:

1. If you're still working and you have an employer-sponsored plan (such as a defined contribution or a defined benefit retirement plan), you may wait until you actually retire before you must take required minimum distributions (RMDs). If you have IRA-based retirement plans (excluding a Roth IRA), you must start taking required minimum distributions as soon as you reach age 70½.
2. If you're not still working, you must take RMDs as soon as you reach age 70½.

The traditional IRA allows you to make tax-deductible contributions to an IRA for your retirement; you will owe tax when you receive distributions from your IRA at retirement.

Roth IRA

We thought we would all be in lower tax brackets when we retired; therefore tax deferral was the plan. However, tax rates are likely to be as high (or even higher) when we retire as when we are working; therefore the benefits of a Roth IRA become more attractive.

A Roth IRA is a retirement plan that allows individuals to make tax-deductible contributions of $4000, to the extent of their earned income. This means individuals may contribute the lesser of income they have earned during a particular tax year *or* $4000. Contributions made to a Roth IRA are made after-tax (meaning they are not tax deductible when made). These contributions, and any growth in the value of the Roth IRA, are tax-free forever.

Under the tax laws applicable to Roth IRAs, your contributions must be made as an individual taxpayer; however, they are *not* taken as a tax deduction on your individual income tax return (Form 1040).

Since its inception in 1997, the Roth IRA (named after its sponsor, Senator William V. Roth Jr. of Delaware) has become a hugely popular investment vehicle. Like the traditional individual retirement account, the Roth IRA is a personal savings plan that offers tax advantages to set aside money for retirement.

Investments in a Roth IRA compound tax deferred, but what provides a unique advantage for the Roth IRA is that, once an individual has reached the age of 59½ and his or her account has existed for more than five years, all withdrawals are tax-free.

Roth IRAs for the taxable year can be opened and/or funded anytime prior to the due date for your individual Form 1040 tax return, excluding extensions. This means anytime prior to April 15 of the calendar year following the tax year in which the deduction is being considered. This due date is applicable to both deductible and nondeductible Roth IRA contributions. Just remember, filing for an extension of time does not extend the time period allowed for contributions.

Earned Income

You can qualify to participate in a retirement plan if you have earned income (compensation) for the tax year in question under the following conditions:

- If you earned profits in your business
- If you paid yourself wages as an employee of your business
- If you paid yourself guaranteed payments—even if your business earned no profits

Contributions

STRATEGY 109

Contribute to your Roth IRA up to a maximum of $4000 annually.

You can contribute up to a maximum of $4000 every year ($4500 if you're age 50 or over), up to the extent of 100 percent of your earned income every year, unless you are prohibited from contributing that year because you generated too much modified adjusted gross income (MAGI) during that year and are therefore subject to the MAGI.

Anyone who has earned income and falls within the MAGI limits can establish a Roth IRA. Unlike the traditional IRA, the Roth IRA has no age limit for contributions, so individuals can continue to contribute as long as they like. (*Note:* In a traditional IRA, individuals can contribute only until age 70½.)

Contributions to a Roth IRA are not tax deductible. Your contribution is made with after-tax dollars. However, the advantage of the Roth IRA is that you will never pay taxes on your earnings or withdrawals (distributions) as long as you have reached the age of 59½ and your account has been open for at least five years. Annual contributions can be taken out at any time with no tax consequences. All other funds (e.g., earnings, conversion funds) can be taken out penalty-free if the account has been established for five years and the individual is over the age of 59½. Noncontribution funds taken out without meeting these requirements are taxable and subject to a 10 percent penalty. Furthermore, there are no mandatory withdrawal requirements, as there are for traditional IRAs.

Modified AGI Limits

STRATEGY 110

Keep an eye on the modified adjusted gross income (MAGI) restrictions when you're making contributions to your Roth IRA.

You may contribute to a Roth IRA if you have taxable compensation and your modified adjusted gross income (MAGI) is less than $110,000 ($160,000 if you are married and file a joint return, and $10,000 if you are married, lived with your spouse, and file a separate return). The amount you may contribute to a Roth IRA is gradually reduced if your modified adjusted gross income is between $95,000 and $110,000 (between $150,000 and $160,000 if you are married and file a joint return, and between $0 and $10,000 if you are married, lived with your spouse, and file a separate return).

The amount you may contribute to a Roth IRA is reduced by contributions you make to a traditional IRA. The amount you may contribute to a Roth IRA also may not exceed your taxable compensation. You may continue to make contributions to your Roth IRA after reaching age 70½.

Distributions

Annual contributions can be taken out at any time with no tax consequence—meaning they are tax-free. Because the contributions you made into your Roth IRA were after-tax, you can withdraw these after tax contributions at any time and pay no income tax. Distributions of accumulated earnings from your Roth IRA are taxable unless you are over age 59½ and have held the account for at least five (5) years.

One further point: There are no mandatory distribution requirements for the Roth IRA. This means that, unlike the traditional IRA, which is subject to required minimum distributions (RMDs), when you reach age 70½ you are not required to make any distributions out of your Roth IRA. This allows you to accumulate your retirement dollars for your future use, and/or for your beneficiaries.

Conversion

STRATEGY 111

Convert your traditional IRA to a Roth IRA when you have many years until retirement.

With a longer time to retirement, you will have the opportunity to maximize the impact of the Roth IRA growing tax-free. Although the contributions to your Roth IRA are made after-tax (non-tax-deductible), any growth in the value of your Roth IRA retirement account accumulates tax-free forever. This tax-free nature of Roth IRAs encourages account owners to consider converting from their traditional IRA accounts to Roth IRAs.

You are allowed to convert amounts from a traditional IRA to a Roth IRA if, for the tax year you make the withdrawal from the traditional IRA, your modified adjusted gross income for Roth IRA purposes is not more than $100,000 and you are not a married individual filing a separate return. The conversion deadline is December 31 of the tax year in which the conversion is to be reported to the IRS, and if your IRA is currently held by another custodian or trustee, instruct that person to convert the traditional IRA to a Roth. When you convert, taxes must be paid on the portion that is being converted; however, you don't have to convert the entire dollar balance, but keep in mind that future growth is tax-free.

Reverse conversion is allowed; if you no longer qualify for a Roth due to unexpected income, you may reverse your conversion, which is termed a *recharacterization*. You have until April 15 or your tax filing deadline, including extensions, to recharacterize your conversion. With a Roth IRA, you are allowed to make contributions past 70½.

The Roth IRA allows you to make after-tax contributions to an IRA for your retirement; these contributed dollars, plus any growth in value, can be distributed to you tax-free at retirement.

CHAPTER 19

Savings Incentive Match Plan for Employees (SIMPLE) IRA

STRATEGY 112

Set up and fund a SIMPLE IRA retirement plan if you want your employees to be able to contribute up to $10,000 annually (of salary-deferral dollars) to a retirement plan—a plan into which you, as the employer, are allowed to make a matching contribution of 3 percent of each employee's annual contribution.

A SIMPLE IRA is a salary-reduction retirement plan that qualifying small employers may offer their employees. Salary-deferral (rather than receiving these amounts as regular salary) contributions of up to $10,000 ($12,000 for individuals age 50 or older) per year may be made by eligible employees, and their employers are required to make matching contributions or a flat contribution. You may contribute the maximum allowable amount to an IRA, as an individual employee, by not receiving the salary you earn when you earn it, but rather by having your employer contribute these amounts directly into your SIMPLE IRA. Another favorable point about this plan is that, as the employer, if you have employees other than your family, you are responsible to match only those funds that the employee contributes first. In addition to these benefits, after two years you may be able to convert your SIMPLE IRA to a Roth IRA.

The Savings Incentive Match Plan for Employees (SIMPLE) was designed as an IRA plan especially for small businesses with 100 or fewer employees. It allows these businesses to offer a tax-advantaged, company-sponsored retirement plan to their employees.

STRATEGY 113

Use the IRS preapproved model for setting up your SIMPLE IRA.

The employer may use a model SIMPLE IRA approved by the IRS to set up a SIM-PLE IRA. Form 5304-SIMPLE allows employees to select a financial institution to which the contributions will be made. Although the employer selects the financial institution to which the contributions are initially deposited, employees have the right to subsequently transfer their account balances without cost or penalty to another financial institution of their own choosing. Use of the IRS model forms is optional; other documents satisfying the statutory requirements for a SIMPLE IRA may be used.

An employer generally may establish a SIMPLE IRA effective on any date between January 1 and October 1 of any tax year and must notify the employees no later than October 1 of the current tax year.

If the employer (or a previous employer) formerly offered a SIMPLE IRA, a new SIMPLE IRA may be effective only on January 1 of a year. A new employer that comes into existence after October 1 of a year may establish a SIMPLE IRA for that year if the plan is established as soon as administratively feasible after the start of the business. Use the IRS preapproved model for setting up your SIMPLE IRA.

A SIMPLE IRA must be set up by or for each eligible employee, and all contributions to the plan must go into these accounts. The employee contribution must be made (by the employer, on behalf of each eligible employee) within 30 days of when these salary-deferred dollars would have been paid to the employee. The employer (matching portion) contribution is due by the due date of the employer's business tax return (including extensions).

Earned Income

You can qualify to participate in a retirement plan if you have earned income (compensation) for the tax year in question under any of the following conditions:

- If you earned profits in your business
- If you paid yourself wages as an employee of your business
- If you paid yourself guaranteed payments—even if your business earned no profits

You are allowed to contribute to your retirement plan the dollar amount of your earned income for the tax year in question, up to the maximum allowed contribution limit for the type of retirement plan you own.

Contributions

STRATEGY 114

Contribute to your SIMPLE IRA up to a maximum salary deferral of $10,000 annually, plus up to 3 percent employer matching portion, annually.

SIMPLE IRA contributions consist of two parts:

Part 1. The first part is a salary-reduction retirement plan whereby the employer (your small business) reduces its employees' salaries in order to create salary-reduction contributions into a SIMPLE IRA for each eligible employee. These contributions are excluded from the employee's taxable W-2 income and are not subject to federal income tax withholding; however, they are subject to the FICA (Social Security and Medicare) tax. This means that each employee's compensation includes a salary reduction up to the amount of his or her annual contribution. Instead of giving employees this portion of their earned income, the employer contributes the dollars into an employer-sponsored SIMPLE IRA. The employer contributes, on behalf of each eligible employee, an amount up to a maximum of $10,000 every year ($12,000 if employees are age 50 or more) up to the extent of their earned income every year. Employees can elect to have up to 100 percent of their annual compensation deferred into their own personal SIMPLE IRA.

Eligible employees must be given notice by the employer of their right to elect salary-reduction contributions and at least 60 days to make the election. After the first year of eligibility, the election to defer for the upcoming year is made during the last 60 days (at a minimum) of the prior calendar year. If the employer uses IRS Form 5304-SIMPLE, a notification document is included.

If an employee contributes to a SIMPLE IRA and also to a 401(k) plan of another employer for the same year, the annual limit on tax-free salary-reduction deferrals ($10,000) applies. Deferrals over the annual limit are taxable and must be removed to avoid being taxed again when distributed from the plan.

Part 2. The second part is a mandatory dollar-for-dollar employer matching portion, whereby the employer matches the employee's salary reduction contribution up to from 1 to 3 percent of each eligible employee's annual compensation.

Each year the employer must make either a matching contribution or a fixed "nonelective" contribution. If the employer chooses matching contributions, the employee's elective salary-reduction contribution (no more than $10,000 or $12,000 for individuals age 50 or older) generally must be matched, up to a limit of 3 percent of the employee's compensation. For up to two years in any five-year period, the 3 percent matching limit may be reduced to as low as 1 percent for each eligible employee.

Instead of making either the 3 percent or reduced limit matching contribution, the employer may make a "nonelective" contribution equal to 2 percent of each eligible employee's contribution. If this option is chosen, the 2 percent contribution must be made for eligible employees whether or not they elect to make salary-reduction contributions for the year. The 2 percent contribution is subject to an annual compensation limit of $170,000. Thus, the maximum 2 percent nonelective contribution is $3400 (2 percent of $170,000) even if an employee earns more than the $170,000. The 3 percent matching contribution is not subject to the annual compensation limit but only to the $10,000 ($12,000 for individuals age 50 or older) salary-reduction limit. The employer must make the matching or nonelective contributions by the due date for filing the employer's tax return (plus extensions) for the year.

With regard to tax deductibility of contributions, employees may deduct their contributions on their personal income tax return (Form 1040), while the employer may deduct the matching amount from the business's taxable income. If you are self-employed, you receive both of these deductions. Remember, you are not allowed to make contributions into your SIMPLE IRA past age 70½.

Employer Eligibility

STRATEGY 115

Make your business eligible to have a SIMPLE IRA retirement plan for your employees.

Generally, any business can establish a SIMPLE IRA retirement plan if it has 100 or fewer employees who earned $5000 or more in compensation during the preceding year and does not concurrently maintain any other employer-sponsored retirement plan.

Remember, for purposes of a SIMPLE IRA, the term *employee* includes a self-employed individual who has earned income. In other words, an owner-employee is both an employer and an employee.

Unlike with regular retirement plans, the nondiscrimination coverage rules do not apply. This means that the plan will qualify even if you as the owner are the only one who elects to participate.

Employee Eligibility

STRATEGY 116

Make your employees eligible to participate in your business's SIMPLE IRA retirement plan.

An employee must be allowed to contribute to a SIMPLE IRA for a year in which he or she is reasonably expected to earn $5000 or more, provided at least $5000 of compensation was received in any two (2) prior years, whether consecutive or not. If the employer owns more than one business and sets up a SIMPLE IRA for one of them, the employees of the other business must also be allowed to participate if they meet the $5000 compensation tests. The employer may lower or eliminate the $5000 compensation requirement in order to broaden participation in the plan. No other conditions or eligibility, such as age or hours of work, are permitted.

STRATEGY 117

Set up a SIMPLE IRA retirement plan for your self-employment side business.

If you are a member of a company retirement plan, you may also set up a SIMPLE IRA for your self-employment side business. For example, if you are an employee of a company that has a qualified 401(k) plan to which you make salary deferrals, you may also set up a SIMPLE IRA plan based on your self-employment earned income. Each plan is independent of the other, and all contributions to a SIMPLE IRA grow tax deferred until they are withdrawn upon your retirement.

Distributions

STRATEGY 118

Avoid the increased penalties for taking distributions from your SIMPLE IRA retirement account during the first two years you own the account.

For the first two years, a higher penalty for distributions before age 59½ applies. The pre-59½ penalty is increased to 25 percent from 10 percent, assuming no penalty exception applies, if the distribution is received during the two-year period starting with the employee's initial participation in the plan. After the first two years, the regular 10 percent penalty applies.

In the initial two-year period, a tax-free rollover or direct trustee-to-trustee transfer of a SIMPLE IRA may be made to another SIMPLE IRA. After the first two years, a tax-free rollover or direct transfer may be made to a regular IRA as well as to a SIMPLE IRA. Keep in mind that no top-heavy rules apply for any year for a SIMPLE IRA.

The methods available for you to take distributions out of your SIMPLE IRA depend on your age and other circumstances.

Under Age 59½

You can take distributions out of your SIMPLE IRA retirement plan if you are under age 59½ using the following methods:

1. Take distributions as part of a "series of substantially equal periodic payments" over the life expectancy of the retirement account owner, or life expectancies of the owner and the beneficiary, using one of the following annuity-type methods:

   a. An annuity purchased by your employer
   b. The "fixed amortization method"
   c. The "fixed annuitization method"

   Under the "series of substantially equal periodic payments" method, the following apply:

   a. Begin at any age, based on a lifetime payout calculation.
   b. Account owner can still be employed.
   c. The "series of substantially equal periodic payments" must continue for a minimum of five (5) years or until the account owner becomes age 59½.

2. Do a rollover into another retirement account.
3. Pay medical expenses in excess of 7.5 percent of your adjusted gross income (AGI).
4. Pay your health insurance if you are unemployed.
5. Take distributions if you are permanently disabled.
6. Take distributions for your higher-education expenses.
7. Take distributions to pay for your first-time home purchase, up to $10,000.

Age 59½ and Older

During this time period, you have considerable discretion in determining the dollar amount of distributions that you will take. If you made tax-deductible (tax-deferred) contributions to your retirement plan, you can take distributions in either of two ways:

1. *The "any dollar amount at any time" method:* Take out any dollar amount you wish whenever you want.
2. *The "lump-sum" method:* Take out the entire balance in your retirement account all at once.

Either way, you are required to pay any and all income tax due on the dollar amount of any distributions you receive in any given tax year—unless "10-year averaging" applies to the lump sum. However, if you made nondeductible (after-tax) contributions to your retirement plan, you can take distributions in any amount at any time and owe no income taxes on these distributions.

Required Minimum Distribution (RMD)

If the sum-total balance of all the account holder's retirement accounts has not been distributed by the account holder's 70½ birthday, the following optional distribution methods apply:

1. If you're still working and you have an employer-sponsored plan (such as a defined contribution or a defined benefit retirement plan), you can wait until you actually retire before you are required to take required minimum distributions (RMDs). If you have IRA-based retirement plans (excluding a Roth IRA), you must start taking required minimum distributions as soon as you reach age 70½.
2. If you're not still working, you must take required minimum distributions as soon as you reach age 70½.

Other Features

Here are several other features unique to SIMPLE IRAs.

Conversion

STRATEGY 119

Convert your SIMPLE IRA into a Roth IRA.

Contributions made to your SIMPLE IRA can be converted into a Roth IRA. The only exception is that withdrawals taken within the first two years of plan participation are not permitted for purposes of conversions to a Roth IRA or rollover/transfer to an IRA other than a SIMPLE IRA.

Your Spouse

STRATEGY 120

Set up a SIMPLE IRA for your spouse if he or she earned $5000 during any of the two preceding calendar years.

A separate SIMPLE IRA is also available to spouses *if* they have received at least $5000 in compensation during any two years preceding the current calendar year and are reasonably expected to earn at least $5000 during the current calendar year in which they are eligible to participate in the plan. They may participate in the plan and open their own SIMPLE IRAs as long as they are employees of the company and meet the income requirements.

Vesting

STRATEGY 121

Treat contributions to employee SIMPLE IRA accounts made by your employees, and contributions made by your business on behalf of its employees, as 100 percent vested immediately.

Employee contributions are immediately 100 percent vested. (The SIMPLE IRAs are owned by the employees themselves.) This means that as soon as your employer makes contributions to your retirement account, these dollars are yours. If you should leave employment with this particular employer and go to work for another business, the balance in your SIMPLE IRA account belongs to you and can be transferred to another retirement account using a trustee-to-trustee transfer.

The SIMPLE IRA allows you to contribute up to $10,000 ($12,000 for individuals age 50 or older) of salary-deferral dollars to your IRA. These dollars accumulate tax deferred until you retire.

CHAPTER 20

Simplified Employee Pension (SEP) IRA

STRATEGY 122

Fund a SEP IRA retirement plan when you want to contribute up to $42,000 annually in pretax dollars to a retirement plan that allows you, as the employer, to make all contributions on behalf of each employee.

A SEP IRA is a retirement plan specifically designed for self-employed people and small-business owners. It's a retirement plan whereby the employer makes contributions on behalf of each employee, and employees may make additional contributions to their SEP IRA that are independent of their employer's contributions. The amount of annual contribution allowed per eligible employee is the lesser of 25 percent of employee compensation up to $210,000, or $42,000 up to the extent of each employee's compensation. The employer must contribute the same percentage of compensation for every eligible employee. This means that the employer may decide whether, and how much, to contribute each tax year. Employers can make contributions to their employees' retirement plans without getting involved in a more complex qualified plan (e.g., regular 401(k)s). If you're self-employed, deductible contributions to your SEP IRA account may not exceed the lesser of 20 percent of your net earnings up to $210,000 (after 50 percent of your net self-employment tax liability) or $42,000, whichever is less.

When you (the employer) do make contributions, they must be based on a specific allocation formula and must not discriminate in favor of yourself, of others who hold more than a 5 percent interest, or of highly compensated employees.

The deadline for both establishing and contributing to a SEP IRA is the tax filing deadline for the company, including extensions. To set up a SEP IRA, you do not need IRS approval. If you do not maintain any other qualified retirement plan, and meet various other requirements, a model SEP may be adopted using Form 5305-SEP. Keep in mind that in addition to your SEP IRA, you can have a traditional IRA.

Earned Income

You can qualify to participate in a retirement plan if you have earned income (compensation) for the tax year in question under any of the following conditions:

- If you earned profits in your business
- If you paid yourself wages as an employee of your business
- If you paid yourself guaranteed payments—even if your business earned no profits

You are allowed to contribute to your retirement plan the dollar amount of your earned income for the tax year in question, up to the maximum allowed contribution limit for the type of retirement plan you own.

Contributions

STRATEGY 123

Contribute to your SEP IRA up to a maximum of $42,000 annually.

A SEP IRA is a retirement plan whereby the employer makes contributions on behalf of each employee. The amount of annual contribution allowed per eligible employee is the lesser of 25 percent of employee compensation up to $210,000, or $42,000 up to the extent of each employee's compensation.

If you are self-employed, deductible contributions to your SEP account may not exceed the lesser of 20 percent of your net earnings up to $210,000 (after 50 percent of your net self-employment tax liability), or $42,000, whichever is less.

STRATEGY 124

Follow these rules for making all SEP IRA contributions.

The following rules apply to all SEP IRA contributions:

1. All SEP IRA contributions must go to traditional IRAs set up for eligible employees.
2. Employers may deduct every qualified dollar they contribute from their business's taxable income.
3. You're not allowed to make contributions past age 70½.
4. Employees are able to exclude from current income the entire dollar amount of the SEP IRA contributions made by their employer on their behalf.
5. An employer is not required to make contributions in any year or to maintain a certain level of contributions into a SEP IRA. This means that employers have the flexibility to change their annual contribution based on the performance of the business.
6. All SEP IRA contributions must be made by the employer using the same percentage of compensation to each eligible employee, including the employer.

Business Eligibility

STRATEGY 125

Make your business eligible to have a SEP IRA retirement plan for your employees.

To take advantage of this strategy, you must be self-employed and your company should have fewer than 25 employees. For purposes of a SEP IRA, the term *employee* includes a self-employed individual who has earned income. In other words, an owner-employee is both an employer and an employee.

Employee Eligibility

> # STRATEGY 126
>
> **Make your employees eligible to participate in your business's SEP IRA retirement plan.**

Employees must be at least 21 years of age, have worked for the business during any three of the past five years, and earned the annual minimum required compensation of $450. Multiple owners and spouses are allowed to participate, and there's no limit on the number of employees that can be covered by an employer.

The ratio of participation of "highly compensated" employees must be close to that of lower-rung workers (though it may be slightly higher). For example, in order for business owners to contribute 6 percent of their salary, the employees must contribute at least 4 percent of their wages to the Solo(k) plan. If the highly paid owners contribute too much relative to the rank-and-file employees, the excess must be returned to the owners (and taxed).

Distributions

The methods available for you to take distributions out of your SEP IRA depend on your age and other circumstances.

Under Age 59½

You can take distributions out of your SEP IRA retirement plan if you are under age 59½ using the following methods:

1. Take distributions as part of a "series of substantially equal periodic payments" over the life expectancy of the retirement account owner, or life expectancies of the owner and the beneficiary, using one of the following annuity-type methods:

   a. An annuity purchased by your employer
   b. The "fixed amortization method"
   c. The "fixed annuitization method"

Under the "series of substantially equal periodic payments" method, the following apply:

    a. Begin at any age, based on a lifetime payout calculation.
    b. Account owner can still be employed.
    c. The "series of substantially equal periodic payments" must continue for a minimum of five (5) years or until the account owner becomes age 59½.

2. Do a rollover into another retirement account.
3. Pay medical expenses in excess of 7.5 percent of your adjusted gross income (AGI).
4. Pay your health insurance if you are unemployed.
5. Take distributions if you are permanently disabled.
6. Take distributions for your higher-education expenses.
7. Take distributions to pay for your first-time home purchase, up to $10,000.

Age 59½ and Older

During this time period, you have considerable discretion in determining the dollar amount of distributions that you will take. If you made tax-deductible (tax-deferred) contributions to your retirement plan, you can take distributions in either of two ways:

1. *The "any dollar amount at any time" method:* Take out any dollar amount you wish whenever you want.
2. *The "lump-sum" method:* Take out the entire balance in your retirement account all at once.

Either way, you are required to pay any and all income tax due on the dollar amount of any distributions you receive in any given tax year—unless "10-year averaging" applies to the lump sum. However, if you made nondeductible (after-tax) contributions to your retirement plan, you can take distributions in any amount at any time and owe no income taxes on these distributions.

Required Minimum Distribution (RMD)

If the sum-total balance of all the account holder's retirement accounts has not been distributed by the account holder's 70½ birthday, the following optional distribution methods apply:

1. If you're still working and you have an employer-sponsored plan (such as a defined contribution or a defined benefit retirement plan), you can wait until you actually

retire before you are required to take required minimum distributions (RMDs). If you have IRA-based retirement plans (excluding a Roth IRA), you must start taking required minimum distributions as soon as you reach age 70½.

2. If you're not still working, you must take required minimum distributions as soon as you reach age 70½.

Other Features

Here are some additional features of SEP IRAs.

Conversion

STRATEGY 127

Convert your SEP IRA into a Roth IRA after you have owned your SEP IRA account for a minimum of two years.

You can convert your SEP IRA into a Roth IRA only if it has been a SEP IRA for a minimum of two (2) years before converting to a Roth IRA. The benefit of this conversion is that your retirement account balance will grow tax-free forever—after you pay any income taxes due upon conversion. Otherwise, the dollars in your SEP IRA will grow tax deferred until you retire, at which time you will owe income tax on any distributions you receive.

Spouse

STRATEGY 128

Create a SEP IRA for your spouse if he or she is an employee of your business.

Spouses may also participate in the plan and open their own SEP IRA as long as they are employed by the company and meet the income requirements. Creating a SEP IRA for your spouse can potentially double both your annual allowed contributions and the totals of your SEP IRA retirement account balances. Your ability to create considerable personal wealth using your retirement accounts just doubled, and the dollar amounts you will enjoy at retirement increase significantly as a direct result of this doubling of your retirement plan efforts.

Vesting

Employee contributions are immediately 100 percent vested. (The SEP IRAs are owned by the employees themselves.) This means that as soon as your employer makes contributions to your retirement account, these dollars are yours. If you should leave employment with this particular employer and go to work for another business, the balance in your SEP IRA account belongs to you and can be transferred to another retirement account using a trustee-to-trustee transfer.

Impact

Contributions to a SEP IRA will not affect the amount an individual can contribute to a traditional IRA or a Roth IRA because the contributions to the SEP IRA are made by the employer rather than by the individual.

Furthermore, if you are a member of an employer-sponsored retirement plan, you may also set up a SEP IRA for your self-employment side business. For example, if you are an employee of a company that has a qualified 401(k) plan into which you make salary deferrals, you may also set up a SEP plan based on your self-employment earned income, as each plan is independent of the other.

The SEP IRA allows you to contribute up to $42,000 of pretax dollars to your IRA. These dollars accumulate tax deferred until your retire.

CHAPTER 21

Qualified Defined Contribution Retirement Plans

Defined contribution plans include profit-sharing and money purchase plans. A separate account must be provided for each employee covered by the plan, and the employee's retirement benefit will be based solely on contributions to the account and its investment gains and earnings.

STRATEGY 129

Understand the details of the dual-contribution matrix applicable to qualified "defined benefit" retirement plans.

Defined benefit retirement plans offer two ways to fund an employee's retirement account:

1. *Profit-sharing plans.* The employer is not required to contribute any particular percentage of profits, but contributions must be sustained and recurring.
2. *Money purchase plans.* An employer's annual contributions are fixed and not based on profits. The employer may be required to contribute a certain percentage of the employee's wages regardless of whether the employer shows a profit for the year.

Under defined contribution plans limits, the annual addition to a participant's account may not exceed the lesser of 100 percent of the participant's compensation (not exceeding $210,000) or $42,000. The term *annual addition* includes employer and employee contributions.

A plan will not qualify unless the annual compensation for each employee taken into account under the plan for any year does not exceed the specific dollar amount of $210,000. If a self-employed person has wages in excess of $210,000, he or she is not qualified to participate in a defined benefit contribution plan.

A defined contribution plan does not fix a specific retirement benefit, but rather sets the amount of annual contributions, so the amount of retirement benefits depends on both contributions and income earned on these contributions.

You are not free to withdraw pension or profit-sharing retirement funds until age 59½ or older; you are subject to a 10 percent penalty for early withdrawal unless you qualify for exemption. *Note:* Pledging your pension or profit-sharing accounts as collateral is treated as a taxable distribution from the account.

There are three types of defined contribution retirement plans:

1. Self-employed 401(k)
2. Regular 401(k)
3. Keogh

The next three sections discuss each of these three plans.

Self-Employed 401(k) Defined Contribution Retirement Plan

STRATEGY 130

Set up and fund a self-employed 401(k) retirement plan if you have no employees and don't expect to have employees (other than yourself) anytime soon.

A self-employed 401(k)—sometimes called a Solo(k), a Solo 401(k), an individual(k), or an individual 401(k)—is for business owners with no full-time employees. However, if the spouses of owners are employees, the business can still qualify for this plan. In addition, your business can be either new or old.

Two components comprise the maximum self-employed 401(k) plan contribution: an owner/employee salary-deferral contribution up to a maximum of $14,000 and an employer profit-sharing contribution up to a maximum of $42,000 (both contribution limits up to the extent of the owner/employee's earned income during the year in which the contribution is made), or a combination of both (not to exceed a total of $42,000), and all contributions are *discretionary*, which means you can elect to contribute or not.

The self-employed 401(k) retirement plan is appropriate only for a business in which solely the owner(s) and spouse(s) will be covered by the plan. It must be the only plan maintained by the business, and the business cannot be considered part of a controlled group under tax law.

The deadline for establishing a self-employed 401(k) plan and for making an employee salary-deferral election is the last day of your business's tax year. The deadline for making both your salary-deferral contribution (as an owner-employee) and an employer (profit-sharing) contribution is the due date of the business's income tax return, including extensions.

Earned Income

You can qualify to participate in a retirement plan if you have earned income (compensation) for the tax year in question under the following conditions:

- If you earned profits in your business
- If you paid yourself wages as an employee of your business
- If you paid yourself guaranteed payments—even if your business earned no profits

You are allowed to contribute to your retirement plan the dollar amount of your earned income for the tax year in question, up to the maximum allowed contribution limit for the type of retirement plan you own.

Contributions

STRATEGY 131

Contribute to your self-employed 401(k) up to a maximum of $42,000 annually.

Contributions to a self-employed 401(k) retirement plan are discretionary (elective). This means you decide each year (1) whether to contribute and (2) how much to contribute—which provides you with complete contribution flexibility.

There is a total contribution limit from both the employee salary-deferral contribution and the employer profit-sharing contribution of $42,000, and income only up to $210,000 can be considered. The maximum total self-employment 401(k) contribution—salary deferral plus profit sharing—that can be contributed is $42,000. An added contribution of up to $4000 in "salary-deferral catch-up" is allowed for those age 50 or older, for a total possible contribution of $46,000. Contributions cannot exceed 100 percent of earned income, and they can be made as soon as the income has been earned.

A self-employed 401(k) consists of two parts: (1) a salary-reduction/deferral part contributed from the employee's wages and (2) a profit-sharing part contributed by the employer from profits. The employee may contribute up to $14,000 through salary deferral, although this may not exceed 100 percent of pay. The employer profit-sharing contribution limit is up to the lesser of $42,000, or 25 percent of your income as an employee, or 20 percent of self-employed income, based on earned income, up to an income limit of $210,000. The total contribution limit from both sources is $42,000.

Part 1: Employee Salary Reduction/Deferral

The first part of the self-employed 401(k) is a salary-reduction retirement plan whereby the employer (i.e., your small business) reduces its employees' salaries up to the amount of each employee's annual contribution to an employer-sponsored self-employed 401(k). The employer may contribute, on behalf of each eligible employee, an amount up to the maximum of $14,000 every year ($18,000 if the employee is age 50 or more) up to the extent of his or her earned income every year.

The maximum that can be contributed from salary deferrals is $14,000, plus up to $4000 catch-up contribution for those age 50 or more, for a total of $18,000. Salary-deferral contributions are pretax and thus reduce the amount of your salary subject to taxes.

Part 2: Employer Profit Sharing

The maximum that can be contributed from the business to your self-employed 401(k) account is 25 percent of your income as an employee or 20 percent of self-employed income, or $42,000, whichever is less. The profit-sharing contribution is not taxed as income to you and is considered a business expense that reduces your business's taxable income. Employees may deduct their contributions from personal taxable income. If you are self-employed, you receive both of these deductions.

Under a self-employed 401(k) retirement plan, an employee typically makes a contribution and the employer usually matches the self-employed 401(k) contribution. Less often, the employer may make all of the self-employed 401(k) contributions. Please note that you are not allowed to make contributions if you are, or your employee is, past age 70½.

Business Eligibility

STRATEGY 132

Make your business eligible to have a self-employed 401(k) retirement plan for your employees.

Self-employed 401(k) plans are appropriate only for a business in which solely the owner(s) and spouse(s) will be covered by the plan. It must be the only plan maintained by the business and the business cannot be considered part of a controlled group under tax law.

Owners and spouses of the owners can be employed by the business; the business cannot have any other employees who work more than 1000 hours per year; and it must be the only plan maintained by the business.

Employee Eligibility

STRATEGY 133

Make your employees eligible to participate in your business's self-employed 401(k) retirement plan.

For purposes of a self-employed 401(k), the term *employee* includes a self-employed individual who has earned income. In other words, an owner-employee is both an employer and an employee. This means that you, as the owner of the business, become eligible for contributions to your self-employed 401(k) for a particular tax year based on the profit of the business, as well as wages the business pays you as an employee, or guaranteed payments you receive (even if the business fails to make a profit for the tax year in question).

Distributions

The methods available for you to take distributions out of your self-employed 401(k) depend on your age and other circumstances. The following sections examine each of these.

Under Age 59½

You can take distributions out of your self-employed 401(k) retirement plan if you are under age 59½ using the following methods:

1. Take distributions as part of a "series of substantially equal periodic payments" over the life expectancy of the retirement account owner, or life expectancies of the owner and the beneficiary, using one of the following annuity-type methods:

   a. An annuity purchased by your employer
   b. The "fixed amortization method"
   c. The "fixed annuitization method"

   Provided:

   a. The account owner has have left the company during or after the calendar year in which you reached age 55.
   b. The account owner has incurred "separation of service" from the employer (has left the company); however, the account owner may still be employed elsewhere.
   c. The "series of substantially equal periodic payments" continues for a minimum of five (5) years, or until the account owner becomes age 59½.

2. Do a rollover into another retirement account.
3. Pay medical expenses in excess of 7.5 percent of your adjusted gross income (AGI).

4. Pay your health insurance if you are unemployed.
5. Take distributions if you are permanently disabled.

Age 59½ and Older

During this time period, you have considerable discretion in determining the dollar amount of distributions that you will take. If you made tax-deductible (tax-deferred) contributions to your retirement plan, you can take distributions in either of two ways:

1. *The "any dollar amount at any time" method:* Take out any dollar amount you wish whenever you want.
2. *The "lump-sum" method:* Take out the entire balance in your retirement account all at once.

Either way, you are required to pay any and all income tax due on the dollar amount of any distributions you receive in any given tax year—unless "10-year averaging" applies to the lump sum. However, if you made nondeductible (after-tax) contributions to your retirement plan, you can take distributions in any amount at any time and owe no income taxes on these distributions.

Required Minimum Distribution (RMD)

If the sum-total balance of all the account holder's retirement accounts has not been distributed by the account holder's 70½ birthday, the following optional allowed distribution methods apply:

1. If you're still working and you have an employer-sponsored plan (such as a defined contribution or a defined benefit retirement plan), you can wait until you actually retire before you are required to take required minimum distributions (RMDs). If you have IRA-based retirement plans (excluding a Roth IRA), you must start taking required minimum distributions as soon as you reach age 70½.
2. If you're not still working, you must take required minimum distributions as soon as you reach age 70½.

Other Features

Several additional features are applicable to self-employed 401(k) defined contribution retirement plans.

Conversion

STRATEGY 134

Convert your self-employed 401(k) account to a SEP IRA account.

If you are self-employed and have no employees, consider opening a self-employed 401(k) at the same time that you open your SEP IRA. You can then request a tax-free rollover of your SEP IRA account into your self-employed 401(k) account. That way you can consolidate your accounts and take advantage of the greater features of the self-employed 401(k), such as its loan feature and its relatively larger contributions as a percentage of pay. Also, you can convert your self-employed 401(k) to a Roth IRA.

Administration

Costs for administration of self-employed plans are generally much lower than those for larger 401(k) plans—about $100 per year. It's easy to set up and inexpensive to maintain, and, unlike with larger 401(k) plans, there are no complicated administrative requirements. You need only to file an IRS Form 5500 when plan assets exceed $100,000.

Because the self-employed 401(k) is designed specifically for businesses that either have no employees or have only employees who may be excluded from coverage testing, it is less complex, less burdensome to administer, and less costly to maintain. The administrator of the plan can be the business owner, his or her spouse or a partner, or a designated third party.

Rollovers

You are allowed to roll over or transfer your traditional IRA, SEP, qualified plans, or Keoghs (profit sharing, money purchase pension, defined benefit), 401(k), 403(b), and governmental 457 plans to an individual(k) plan. SIMPLE IRAs are eligible for rollover after the two-year holding period.

You may roll over or transfer to your self-employed 401(k) funds from other retirement accounts or pension plans—including IRA, SEP, TSP, 457, and Keogh plans.

Transfers

You can transfer any amount from other pretax retirement funds into your self-employed 401(k) account, and you may borrow from it. The logic behind this is to be able to obtain a loan from your retirement account when your current plan doesn't allow it. All you have to do is initiate a trustee-to-trustee transfer from your current retirement plan account (that doesn't allow loans) into your self-employed 401(k) account and then borrow from it.

Loan

STRATEGY 135

Borrow money from your self-employed 401(k) account balance.

You are allowed to borrow money from your self-employed 401(k) account balance. You can take a loan from the plan if specifically allowed under the plan documents. You must provide collateral (which can be done by pledging the balance of your own self-employed 401(k) account, and you may borrow up to 50 percent of your account balance, or $50,000, whichever is less. Generally you must repay the loan, with interest, at commercial loan rates, within five (5) years. Repayment period and interest rate are subject to IRS guidelines. The loan interest rate is fixed at prime at the time that you borrow. Loan payments and interest on loans go back to your self-employed 401(k). Loans are tax-free and penalty-free as long as the loan is paid back on time; if you fail to repay the loan according to the terms and conditions of the loan, the loan becomes taxable income to you. *Note:* For home purchases or home improvements, you may extend the repayment schedule to 30 years.

Spouses

STRATEGY 136

Create a self-employed 401(k) for your spouse if he or she is an employee of your business.

Spouses are eligible to open their own self-employed 401(k) account as long as they are employed by the company and covered by the plan. Creating a self-employed 401(k) for your spouse can potentially double your annual allowed contributions and the totals of your self-employed 401(k) retirement account balances. Your ability to create considerable personal wealth using your retirement accounts just doubled, and the dollar amounts you will enjoy at retirement increase significantly as a direct result of this doubling of your retirement plan efforts.

Allowed contributions to your self-employed 401(k) retirement plan consist of two components: (1) up to $14,000 in salary deferral and (2) up to $42,000 from your employer in profit sharing. *Note:* the combination of salary deferrals plus employer profit sharing must not exceed the $42,000 limit.

Regular 401(k) Defined Contribution Retirement Plan

STRATEGY 137

Set up and fund a regular 401(k) retirement plan if you own a larger business, with 20 or more employees.

Employer contributions to plans of this type are not to be included in the income of a participant because (1) the employee has the option of taking the contributions in cash or having them paid to the plan (an *elective contribution*), or (2) the contribution coincides with a salary-reduction arrangement.

As a general rule, matching contributions made to a 401(k) plan by the employer are not treated as an employee's elective contributions and are, therefore, not subject to the annual limit of $14,000. Keep in mind that matching contributions made to 401(k) plans for self-employed persons are not treated as part of the individual's elective contributions.

The regular 401(k) is designed for larger businesses, those with 20 or more employees. Contributions, up to $14,000 annually, are made by the employee using salary deferral up to the extent of the employee's compensation; and the employer can also make a contribution (on behalf of each eligible employee) of the lesser of $42,000 or 25 percent of the employee's compensation up to $210,000.

You must formally set up a regular 401(k) plan before the end of the tax year in which you want the plan to be effective. Contributions must be made by the due date of the business's income tax return, including extensions.

If you establish a 401(k) plan, the following apply:

- You can have other retirement plans.
- You can own a business of any size.
- You need to file Form 5500 annually.

You can make a regular 401(k) plan as simple or as complex as you want to. A preapproved regular 401(k) plan might be just the thing if you want to cut down on administrative headaches and expenses.

With a regular 401(k) plan, employees can choose to defer some of their salary. Instead of receiving that amount in their paycheck, they defer, or delay, getting that money. In this case, their deferred money is going into a regular 401(k) plan sponsored by their employer (that would be you). This deferred money generally does not get taxed by the federal government or by most state governments until it is distributed.

A regular 401(k) plan offers the maximum flexibility of the three types of plans. Employers have discretion to make contributions on behalf of all participants, to match employees' deferrals, or do both. These contributions can be subject to a vesting schedule, which means that an employee's right to employer contributions becomes nonforfeitable only after a certain period of time. In addition, a regular 401(k) allows participants to make pretax contributions through payroll deductions. Annual testing ensures that benefits for rank-and-file employees are proportional to benefits for owners/managers.

Before beginning a plan document, however, you will need to decide on the type of 401(k) plan that is best for you: a regular 401(k), a safe harbor 401(k), or a SIMPLE 401(k) plan.

Earned Income

You can qualify to participate in a retirement plan if you have earned income (compensation) for the tax year in question under the following conditions:

- If you earned profits in your business
- If you paid yourself wages as an employee of your business
- If you paid yourself guaranteed payments—even if your business earned no profits

You are allowed to contribute to your retirement plan the dollar amount of your earned income for the tax year in question, up to the maximum allowed contribution limit for the type of retirement plan you own.

Contributions

STRATEGY 138

Contribute to your self-employed 401(k) up to a maximum of $42,000 annually.

The regular 401(k) is designed for the larger businesses, with 20 or more employees. Contributions are made by the employee, using a salary deferral, up to $14,000 annually ($18,000 if age 50 or older) up to the extent of the employee's compensation; the employer can also make a contribution (on behalf of each eligible employee) of the lesser of $42,000 or 25 percent of the employee's compensation up to $210,000.

Total employer and employee contributions to all of an employer's plans are subject to an overall annual limitation based on the lesser of 100 percent of the employee's compensation up to $210,000 *or* $42,000. Please note, though, that you are not allowed to make contributions past age 70½.

If you decide to contribute to your employees' regular 401(k) accounts, you have further options. You can contribute a percentage of each employee's compensation to the employee's account (called a *nonelective contribution*), or you can match the amount your employees decide to contribute (within the limits of current law), or you can do both.

For example, you may decide to add a percentage—say 50 percent—to an employee's contribution, which results in a 50-cent increase for every dollar the employee sets aside. Using a matching-contribution formula will provide additional employer contributions only to employees who make deferrals to the regular 401(k) plan. If you choose to make nonelective contributions, the employer makes a contribution to each eligible participant's account, whether or not the participant decides to make a salary deferral to his or her regular 401(k) account.

Under a regular 401(k) plan, you may have the flexibility of changing the amount of nonelective contributions each year depending on business conditions.

Two Additional Opportunities

Within the regular 401(k) family of retirement plans are two additional strategies you can follow, described in this section.

Safe Harbor 401(k) Plan

Under a safe harbor plan, you can match each eligible employee's contribution, dollar for dollar, up to 3 percent of the employee's compensation, and up to 50 cents on the dollar for the employee's contribution that exceeds 3 percent, but does not exceed 5 percent, of the employee's compensation. Alternatively, you can make a nonelective contribution equal to 3 percent of an employee's compensation to each eligible employee's account. Each year you must choose either the matching contributions or the nonelective contributions.

A safe harbor 401(k) plan is similar to a regular 401(k) plan, but, among other things, it must provide for employer contributions that are fully vested when made. However, the safe harbor 401(k) is not subject to many of the complex tax rules that are associated with a regular 401(k) plan, including annual nondiscrimination testing.

SIMPLE 401(k) plan

A SIMPLE 401(k) plan may be established by an employer who has 100 or fewer employees who received at least $5000 in compensation from the employer for the preceding year. The employer must not maintain any other retirement plan, and each eligible employee must have the right to make an annual elective contribution, which is expressed as a percentage of compensation, not to exceed $10,000.

Employer contributions to a SIMPLE 401(k) plan are limited to either a dollar-for-dollar matching contribution, up to 3 percent of pay, *or* a nonelective contribution of 2 percent of pay for each eligible employee.

No other employer contributions can be made to a SIMPLE 401(k) plan, and employees cannot participate in any other retirement plan of the employer. The maximum amount that employees can contribute to their SIMPLE 401(k) accounts is $10,000.

SIMPLE 401(k) plans were created so that small businesses could have a cost-efficient way to offer retirement benefits to their employees. SIMPLE 401(k) plans are not subject to the annual nondiscrimination tests that apply to traditional plans. Similarly to a safe harbor 401(k) plan, the employer is required to make contributions that are fully vested. This type of 401(k) plan is available to employers with 100 or fewer employees who received at least $5000 in compensation from the employer for the preceding calendar year. In addition, employees who are covered by a SIMPLE 401(k) plan may not receive any contributions or benefit accruals under any other plans of the employer.

Once you have decided on the type of plan for your company, you will have flexibility in choosing some of the plan's features, such as which employees may contribute to the plan and how much. Other features written into the plan are required by law. For instance, the plan document must describe how certain key functions are carried out, such as how contributions are deposited in the plan.

Combination

Both regular 401(k) and safe harbor 401(k) plans are for employers of any size and can be combined with other retirement plans. The contributions include both employee salary deferrals and/or employer contributions.

Distributions

The methods available for you to take distributions out of these retirement accounts—regular 401(k)s, safe harbor 401(k)s, or SIMPLE 401(k)s—depend on your age and other circumstances.

Under Age 59½

You can take distributions out of your regular 401(k) retirement plan if you are under age 59½ using the following methods:

1. Take distributions as part of a "series of substantially equal periodic payments" over the life expectancy of the retirement account owner, or life expectancies of the owner and the beneficiary, using one of the following annuity-type methods:

    a. An annuity purchased by your employer
    b. The "fixed amortization method"
    c. The "fixed annuitization method"

    Provided:

    a. The account owner has have left the company during or after the calendar year in which you reached age 55.

 b. The account owner has incurred "separation of service" from the employer (has left the company); however, the account owner may still be employed elsewhere.

 c. The "series of substantially equal periodic payments" continues for a minimum of five (5) years, or until the account owner becomes age 59½.

2. Do a rollover into another retirement account.
3. Pay medical expenses in excess of 7.5 percent of your adjusted gross income (AGI).
4. Pay your health insurance if you are unemployed.
5. Take distributions if you are permanently disabled.

Age 59½ and Older

During this time period, you have considerable discretion in determining the dollar amount of distributions that you will take.

If you made tax-deductible (tax-deferred) contributions to your retirement plan, you can take distributions in either of two ways:

1. *The "any dollar amount at any time" method:* Take out any dollar amount you wish whenever you want.
2. *The "lump-sum" method:* Take out the entire balance in your retirement account all at once.

Either way, you are required to pay any and all income tax due on the dollar amount of any distributions you receive in any given tax year—unless "10-year averaging" applies to the lump sum. However, if you made nondeductible (after-tax) contributions to your retirement plan, you can take distributions in any amount at any time and owe no income taxes on these distributions.

Required Minimum Distribution (RMD)

If the sum-total balance of all the account holder's retirement accounts has not been distributed by the account holder's 70½ birthday, the following optional allowed distribution methods apply:

1. If you're still working and you have an employer-sponsored plan (such as a defined contribution or a defined benefit retirement plan), you can wait until you actually

retire before you are required to take required minimum distributions (RMDs). If you have IRA-based retirement plans (excluding a Roth IRA), you must start taking required minimum distributions as soon as you reach age 70½.

2. If you're not still working, you must take required minimum distributions as soon as you reach age 70½.

Other Features

Several additional features are applicable to regular 401(k) defined contribution plans.

Administration

STRATEGY 139

Comply with the considerable administrative and filing requirements of the regular 401(k) retirement plan.

Once you have established a regular 401(k) plan, you assume certain responsibilities in operating the plan. If you hire someone to help in setting up your plan, that arrangement also may include help in operating the plan. If not, another important decision will be whether to manage the plan yourself or hire a professional or financial institution to take care of some or most aspects of operating the plan. Here are some elements of a plan that need to be handled:

- Filing an annual report with the federal government (Form 5500, Annual Return/Report of Employee Benefit Plan, or Form 5500-EZ, Annual Return of One-Participant (Owners and Their Spouses) Retirement Plan
- Filing a Form 1099-R, Distributions from Pensions, Annuities, Retirement or Profit-Sharing Plans, IRAs, Insurance Contracts, etc.
- Summary plan description (SPD).
- Summary of material modification (SMM)

- Individual benefit statement (IBS)
- Summary annual report (SAR)

Participation

STRATEGY 140

Understand and apply the participation requirements for employees and employer-owners of your business.

Typically, a plan benefits a mix of rank-and-file employees and employer-owners; however, some employees may be excluded from a 401(k) plan under the following conditions:

- They have not attained age 21.
- They have not completed a year of service.
- They are covered by a collective bargaining agreement that does not provide for participation in the plan if retirement benefits were the subject of good faith bargaining.

Note that employees cannot be excluded from a plan merely because they are older workers.

Vesting

In regular 401(k) plans, all employee salary deferrals are 100 percent vested. This means that the money that an employee has put aside through salary deferrals cannot be forfeited. When an employee leaves a company, he or she is entitled to those deferrals, plus any investment gains (or losses) on those deferrals. Employer contributions may be vested on a graduated vesting schedule. In safe harbor 401(k) plans and SIMPLE 401(k) plans, all required employer contributions are always 100 percent vested. You can design your plan so that employer contributions become vested over time, according to a specified vesting schedule.

Loans

STRATEGY 141

Borrow money from your regular 401(k) for any use whatsoever and pay yourself back, with interest.

You can borrow dollars from your 401(k) retirement account under very specific rules and regulations. These rules vary somewhat depending on the details of your plan; however, most plans do allow you to borrow up to 50 percent of your account balance and repay this loan, plus interest, to yourself monthly over a specific number of months.

You are allowed to use these dollars as you see fit; as long as you repay the loan under the agreed-upon terms and conditions, you will not have to pay the 10 percent tax penalty plus any ordinary income tax due. However, if you default on a loan from your regular 401(k) plan, you are considered to have received a distribution from your plan; in that case, whether you will have to pay the 10 percent tax penalty or any income tax due depends on your age when the loan was converted into a distribution.

Establish and use a regular 401(k) defined contribution retirement plan only if you are a larger business, with 20 or more employees. You may use a combination of employee salary deferrals plus profit sharing from your business.

Keogh Defined Contribution Retirement Plan

STRATEGY 142

Set up and fund a Keogh defined contribution retirement plan if you are self-employed and want to make the maximum allowable contributions based on your current tax year's earned income.

The Keogh defined contribution retirement plan was designed for self-employed individuals who function as both the employer and an employee; therefore, for purposes of a Keogh, the term *employee* includes a self-employed individual who has earned income. In other words, an owner-employee is both an employer and an employee.

If you are a member of a company retirement plan, you may also set up a Keogh defined contribution retirement plan for your self-employment side business. For example, if you are an employee of a company that has a qualified 401(k) plan to which you make salary deferrals, you may also set up a Keogh defined contribution retirement plan based on your self-employment earned income.

Contributions are made into a Keogh defined contribution retirement plan based on the earned income of the account owner during the tax year in question, up to a maximum of the lesser of 100 percent of compensation up to $210,000, or $42,000.

STRATEGY 143

Set up a defined contribution Keogh retirement plan for your self-employment side business.

If you are a member of a company retirement plan, you may also set up a Keogh defined contribution retirement plan for your self-employment side business. For example, if you are an employee of a company that has a qualified 401(k) plan to which you make salary deferrals, you may also set up a Keogh plan based on your self-employment earned income.

Setup

STRATEGY 144

Set up your Keogh defined contribution retirement plan without advance IRS approval.

You may set up your own Keogh defined contribution retirement plan and contribute to it without advance approval. If you do wish to obtain advance approval, you may do so by requesting approval directly from the IRS. Approval requirements depend on whether you set up your own plan or join a master plan administered by a bank, an insurance company, a mutual fund, or a prototype plan sponsored by a trade or professional association. If you start our own individually designed plan, you'll need to apply for a determination letter on Form 5300.

You must formally set up a defined contribution Keogh plan before the end of the tax year in which you want the plan to be effective. Contributions are due by the due date of the business's income tax return (including extensions). Excess contributions may be carried over and deducted in later years, subject to the ceiling for those years. However, excess contributions are generally subject to a 10 percent penalty on nondeductible contributions that are not returned by the end of the tax year.

Creating Earned Income (Compensation)

STRATEGY 145

Consider the unique earned income qualification requirements under a Keogh defined contribution retirement plan.

Unlike other retirement plans, a Keogh defined contribution retirement plan does not recognize W-2 wages paid to the owner as earned income. This means these W-2 wages cannot be used to qualify you to make contributions to your Keogh. For Keogh plans, earned income is generated only by the sources listed in Table 21.1, depending on your form of business organization.

Table 21.1   Sources of Earned Income for Keogh Plans

Sole Proprietorship
- Bottom-line profit

One-Member LLC
- Taxed as a sole proprietorship: Bottom-line profit

Partnership*
- Pro rata share of bottom-line profit
- Guaranteed payments (even if partnership doesn't make any profit)

Limited Partnership
- General partner

    Pro rata share of bottom-line profit

    Guaranteed payments (even if partnership doesn't make any profit)

- Limited partner(s): Guaranteed payments (even if partnership doesn't make any profit)

Multiple-Member LLC†
- Taxed as a sole partnership: Pro rata share of bottom-line profit

*Partnership plans: An individual partner or partners, although self-employed, may not set up a Keogh plan; the Keogh plan must be established by the partnership. Partnership deductions for contributions to an individual partner's account are reported on the partner's Schedule K-1 (Form 1065) and deducted by the partner as an adjustment to income on line 29 of his or her own individual tax return (Form 1040).
†Members of a multiple-owner LLC, although self-employed, may not set up a Keogh plan; the Keogh plan must be established by the LLC. LLC deductions for contributions to an individual partner's account are reported on the member's Schedule K-1 (Form 1065) and deducted by the member as an adjustment to income on line 29 of his or her own individual tax return (Form 1040).

Contributions

> # STRATEGY 146
>
> **Make contributions to your Keogh defined contribution retirement plan using contributions from your profit-sharing plan, your money purchase plan, or a paired plan (combination of profit-sharing and money purchase) up to $42,000 annually.**

Contributions are due by the due date of the business's income tax return (including extensions), and they are tax deductible to the business. No employee contributions are allowed; all contributions are made by the employer. Additionally, you are not allowed to make contributions for yourself or an employee if past age 70½.

The maximum contribution that can be made to a defined contribution Keogh retirement plan is the lesser of 100 percent of compensation up to $210,000, or $42,000. This total contribution can be made in one of three ways: (1): a profit-sharing contribution, plus (2) a money purchase contribution, the total of which, (1) plus (2), may not exceed the lesser of 100 percent of compensation up to $210,000, or $42,000 annually, or (3): a paired contribution, which is a combination of (1) and (2):

1. *Profit-sharing plan.* Contributions to the plan are contingent on your business having profit from which to pay the contributions. You can contribute up to 20 percent of your earnings from self-employment, up to a maximum of $42,000 per year. A profit-sharing plan does allow the use of vesting schedules and Social Security integration (not allowed by SEP IRA plans), and you don't have to make a contribution every year.
2. *Money purchase plan.* A plan that requires fixed contributions regardless of your business profits—even if you have a loss. You can contribute more to these plans than you can to either a profit-sharing plan or a SEP IRA. As an owner, you can contribute the lesser of 100 percent of your self-employment income or $42,000 per year. This allows for a larger contribution; however, *no* flexibility is allowed on the percentage of contributions you make each year. This feature makes this plan better suited for high-income earners who are comfortable enough financially to know they can continue making large-percentage contributions.

Note that the maximum deduction percentage for regular employees under a Keogh defined contribution money purchase plan is 25 percent of their wages.

3. *Paired plan.* A plan that combines the profit-sharing plan and the money purchase plan. You can attain the maximum contribution possible (100 percent) that you can get (as an owner) with the money purchase pension plan, but you have some of the flexibility that comes with a profit-sharing plan. For example, you can fix your money purchase pension plan contributions at 80 percent and contribute anywhere from 0 to 20 percent of your net income to your profit-sharing plan. Thus, in any given plan year, you may contribute as little as 0 percent of your net income or as much as 20 percent.

Business Eligibility

STRATEGY 147

Make your business eligible to have a Keogh defined contribution retirement plan for your employees.

You may make your business eligible for a Keogh defined contribution plan participation by setting up the plan and contributing to it without any advance approval. However, since advanced approval is advisable, you may, in your determination letter, ask the IRS to review your plan. Approval requirements depend on whether you administer your own plan or join a master plan administered by a bank, an insurance company, a mutual fund, or a prototype plan sponsored by a trade or professional association. If you start your own individually designed plan, you may apply for a determination letter on Form 5300 (whether the plan is defined benefit or defined contribution). You must pay a fee to the IRS when you apply for a determination letter. File Form 8717, showing your fee, along with Form 5300.

Employee Eligibility (Inclusion)

STRATEGY 148

Apply the inclusion rules for making your employees eligible for participation in your Keogh defined contribution retirement plan.

In order for your employees to be eligible to participate in a Keogh defined benefit retirement plan, your plan must meet the following conditions:

- You must include in your plan all employees who have reached age 21 and who have at least one year of service. An employee may be required to complete two years of service before participating in your plan if your plan provides for full membership and immediate vesting after no more than two years. You are generally not required to cover seasonal or part-time employees who work less than 1000 during a 12-month period.
- You may not exclude employees who are over a certain age.
- You may not discriminate in favor of officers or other highly compensated personnel.
- You must provide benefits for the employees and their beneficiaries, and their plan rights may not be subject to forfeiture.
- You may not allow any of the funds to be diverted for purposes other than pension benefits.
- You may not receive contributions made on your behalf that exceed the ratio of contributions made on behalf of employees.

Top-Heavy Rules

STRATEGY 149

Incorporate the IRS top-heavy rules when making contributions under a Keogh defined contribution retirement plan.

The top-heavy rules apply if more than 60 percent of a Keogh defined contribution plan account balances, or more than 60 percent of the accrued benefits, are for key employees. These include employees who at any time during the plan year own one of the 10 largest ownership interests and have annual compensation exceeding $30,000 *or* have more than a 5 percent interest in the company *or* have more than a 1 percent interest and also receive annual compensation of more than $150,000.

Officers are considered key employees if they receive annual compensation exceeding $65,000, and key employee treatment is also applicable to employees who were key employees in any of the four preceding years under the applicable compensation limit for each such year.

Even if your pension or profit-sharing plans are not currently considered top-heavy, your plans may be disqualified unless they include provisions that would automatically take effect if the plans were to become top-heavy. The major top-heavy restriction requires an accelerated vesting schedule.

A top-heavy plan must provide either 100 percent vesting after three years of service *or* graded vesting at the rate of at least 20 percent after two years of service, 40 percent after three years of service, 60 percent after four years of service, 80 percent after five years of service, and 100 percent after six years of service. (The "100 percent vesting after three years of service" may be a better option if your business has a high turnover rate.)

The first $170,000 of a self-employed person's earned income is used to determine whether the plan is top-heavy.

Distributions

The methods available for you to take distributions out of your Keogh defined contribution retirement plan depend on your age and other circumstances.

Under Age 59½

You can take distributions out of your Keogh defined contribution retirement plan if you are under age 59½ using the following methods:

1. Take distributions as part of a "series of substantially equal periodic payments" over the life expectancy of the retirement account owner, or life expectancies of the owner and the beneficiary, using one of the following annuity-type methods:

    a. An annuity purchased by your employer
    b. The "fixed amortization method"

c. The "fixed annuitization method"

Provided:

a. The account owner has left the company during or after the calendar year in which you reached age 55.

b. The account owner has incurred "separation of service" from the employer (i.e., has left the company); however, the account owner may still be employed elsewhere.

c. The "series of substantially equal periodic payments" continues for a minimum of five years, or until the account owner becomes age 59½.

2. Do a rollover into another retirement account.
3. Pay medical expenses in excess of 7.5 percent of your adjusted gross income (AGI).
4. Pay your health insurance if you are unemployed.
5. Take distributions if you are permanently disabled.

Age 59½ and Older

During this time period, you have considerable discretion in determining the dollar amount of distributions that you will take.

If you made tax-deductible (tax-deferred) contributions to your retirement plan, you can take distributions in either of two ways:

1. *The "any dollar amount, at any time" method:* Take out any dollar amount you wish whenever you want.
2. *The "lump-sum" method:* Take out the entire balance in your retirement account all at once.

Either way, you are required to pay any and all income tax due on the dollar amount of any distributions you receive in any given tax year—unless "10-year averaging" applies to the lump sum. However, if you made nondeductible (after-tax) contributions to your retirement plan, you can take distributions in any amount at any time and owe no income taxes on these distributions.

Required Minimum Distribution (RMD)

If the sum-total balance of all the account holder's retirement accounts has not been distributed by the account holder's 70½ birthday, the following optional allowed distribution methods apply:

1. If you're still working and you have an employer-sponsored plan, you can wait until you actually retire before you are required to take required minimum distributions (RMDs). If you have IRA-based retirement plans (excluding a Roth IRA), you must start taking required minimum distributions as soon as you reach age 70½.
2. If you're not still working, you must take required minimum distributions as soon as you reach age 70½.

Other Features

Here are additional features applicable to Keogh defined contribution plans.

Administration

The annual Keogh defined contribution plan return is due on July 31 of the year following the plan tax year (unless an extension is obtained from the IRS). Use Form 5500-EZ for one-participant plans (including yourself and your spouse if you are a sole proprietorship or a one-person LLC), or if you and your business partners/members and spouses are operating as either a partnership or a multiple-member LLC in which the only plan participants are partners/members and their spouses). You must file a Form 5500-EZ for the first year the assets of your plan exceed $100,000 and for each year thereafter, even if the plan's total assets drop below the $100,000 threshold (temporarily or permanently).

If you cannot file Form 5500-EZ, you must file Form 5500-C/R if there are fewer than 100 plan participants (Form 5500 if there are 100 or more participants).

Controlled Groups

STRATEGY 150

Aggregate your Keogh defined contribution funds from more than one business to avoid violating the "controlled group" limitations.

Multiple businesses owned by the same individual(s) are called a *controlled group;* under these circumstances, the businesses are aggregated for purposes of the limitation applied to defined benefits. If you have more than one business, you cannot set up separate Keogh defined contribution accounts to avoid the applicable annual dollar limits on contributions.

Vesting

Defined contribution Keogh retirement plans allow vesting schedules, which require employees to remain with the business for a specified number of years before they earn the right to their full retirement account balances. *Vesting* refers to the portion of the retirement account dollars that the employer owns. After a certain number of years, employees becomes "fully vested" and therefore own 100 percent of their share of the funds. If an employee leaves prior to becoming fully vested, he or she loses the unvested balance, which reverts to the remaining plan participants on a pro rata basis.

Loans

STRATEGY 151

Borrow money from your Keogh defined contribution retirement plan carefully to avoid the prohibited-transition penalties.

Owner-employee Keogh defined contribution plan loans to an owner-employee (more than 10 percent ownership) are subject to prohibited-transaction penalties. There are two penalties: (1) a 15 percent first-tier penalty and (2) a 100 percent penalty. The 15 percent penalty applies to the year of the loan and later years until the loan is repaid with interest. The penalty is figured on a fair-market interest factor. The 100 percent penalty is imposed if the loan is not repaid. The penalty may be avoided by repaying the loan within 90 days after the IRS sends a deficiency notice for the 100 percent tax. If you are an owner-employee, you may be able to apply to the Department of Labor for a special exemption from the prohibited-transaction penalties.

Prohibitions

The following restrictions apply to Keogh defined contribution plans:

- They cannot be converted to Roth.
- They cannot be self-directed.
- Nondeductible contributions are not allowed.
- Note: Owner can have more than one business, but only one business can have a Keogh plan.

A Keogh defined contribution retirement plan is specifically set up for self-employed individuals. Contributions are made to a Keogh defined contribution plan based on the earned income of the account owner during the tax year in question, up to a maximum of the lesser of (1) 100 percent of compensation up to $210,000 or (2) $42,000.

CHAPTER 22

Qualified Defined Benefit Retirement Plans

Defined benefit plans include pension and annuity plans that offer a specific retirement benefit to employees. The benefit is usually in the form of a monthly retirement pension that is based on the employee's wages and years of service with the employer. An employer's annual contributions to the plan are based on actuarial assumptions and are not allocated to individual accounts maintained for the employees.

For defined benefit plans only, a minimum coverage rule requires that the plan must include at least 40 percent of all employees (or 50 employees, if that is less).

The following are two types of defined benefit retirement plans:

1. Solo-DB
2. Keogh

The next two sections will cover each of these plans in depth.

Solo-DB Individual Defined Benefit Retirement Plan

STRATEGY 152

Set up and fund a Solo-DB (defined benefit) retirement plan if you wish to contribute up to a maximum of $170,000 annually to your retirement plan.

The Solo-DB retirement plan is designed to offer specific dollar benefits to the account owner at retirement. It's a qualified retirement plan in which you set a target monthly or annual dollar benefit that you want to receive when you retire. Your annual contributions to the plan are calculated taking into account your current age, the average of your three highest years of income, your planned retirement age, and, in subsequent years, balances you have accumulated in the plan. Annual contributions are mandatory, and a higher targeted benefit will result in greater required annual contributions.

It offers the largest tax-deductible retirement contribution permitted by law, functioning as a slimmed down "one-person" version of the defined benefit (DB) pension plans commonly found at large corporations. The small-business client gets a business deduction for his or her contribution to the plan, which allows that individual to put away up to $170,000 a year for retirement while getting a full tax deduction for that contribution.

Unlike profit-sharing plans, which allow a business owner to cease payments at his or her discretion, contributions to defined benefit plans are mandatory. This means the client needs a constant stream of high income to ensure funding.

The Solo-DB plans are a bit restrictive in that most are set up requiring them to last a minimum of five to seven years, up to a minimum of 10 years' worth of contributions. Furthermore, the IRS requires that a business offering this benefit to one person must make it available to all.

The Solo-DB account owner must be a high-net-worth individual who can afford a minimum annual maintenance fee of approximately $1500. The fees on some plans could be as high as $7000 a year or more, since actuarial approval is needed annually.

A Solo-DB is a defined benefit retirement plan with a maximum annual contribution of up to $170,000. It's designed for the successful small-business owner whose business has stable income, whose business has (ideally) been in existence for three or more years, and who is willing to make ongoing mandatory annual contributions of more than $42,000 per year (up to $170,000 per year), typically for a minimum period of three consecutive years. Note that some Solo-DB plans require mandatory annual contributions for a minimum of anywhere from 5 to 10 consecutive years. The largest contributions go to the older and more highly compensated employees, who tend to be the business owners.

The Solo-DB plan is designed for older business owners who have no employees (the limit is four), unless the employees are partners in the business or spouses of the owners. With a Solo-DB plan, you set a target dollar benefit that you want to receive when you retire. An actuary calculates your required annual contributions to the plan based on your target benefit, age, income, planned retirement age, and how much you have in the plan. These calculations are designed to create a plan that has an adequate amount of dollars (at the time of your retirement) to pay a specific (defined) benefit to you upon your retirement.

Setup

The due date for establishing a Solo-DB retirement plan is the last day of the business's tax year. Contributions must be made by your business's tax filing deadline for the tax year, plus any extensions, but no later than September 15.

Earned Income

STRATEGY 153

Generate earned income for your Solo-DB retirement plan from three distinct sources.

You can qualify to participate in a retirement plan if you have earned income (compensation) for the tax year in question under the following three conditions:

1. If you earned profits in your business
2. If you paid yourself wages as an employee of your business
3. If you paid yourself guaranteed payments—even if your business earned no profits

You are allowed to contribute to your retirement plan the dollar amount of your earned income for the tax year in question, up to the maximum allowed contribution limit for the type of retirement plan you own.

Contributions

STRATEGY 154

Contribute up to $170,000 annually to your Solo-DB retirement plan.

For the ultimate in tax-deductible contributions, no retirement plan beats the defined benefit plan. Depending on your circumstances, you may be able to contribute in excess of $170,000 per year to such a plan, and you may exclude from the plan any employee who works fewer than 1000 hours per year.

You must contribute to your Solo-DB plan every year; however, the plan benefit formula can be amended for future years, resulting in an increase or decrease of the required contribution amount. Depending on when you amend the plan, you may still be required to make the contribution for the current year.

A business owner may have more than one source of money, but in no event can the business owner deduct more than the net income generated from the business that is sponsoring the plan.

Each year you may be required to put more or less money into the plan to achieve your goal, depending on whether the plan's investments under- or overperform the hypothetical rate of return that was used to calculate your annual contribution amount. Remember, you are not allowed to make contributions past age 70½.

Distribution

You can take distributions out of your Solo-DB retirement plan if you are under age 59½ using the methods discussed in this section.

Under Age 59½

You can take distributions out of your self-employed 401(k) retirement plan if you are under age 59½ using the following methods:

1. Take distributions as part of a "series of substantially equal periodic payments" over the life expectancy of the retirement account owner, or life expectancies of the owner and the beneficiary, using one of the following annuity-type methods:

   a. An annuity purchased by your employer
   b. The "fixed amortization method"
   c. The "fixed annuitization method"

   Provided:

   a. The account owner has left the company during or after the calendar year in which you reached age 55.
   b. The account owner has incurred "separation of service" from the employer (has left the company); however, the account owner may still be employed elsewhere.

   c. The "series of substantially equal periodic payments" continues for a minimum of five (5) years, or until the account owner becomes age 59½.
  2. Do a rollover into another retirement account.
  3. Pay medical expenses in excess of 7.5 percent of your adjusted gross income (AGI).
  4. Pay your health insurance if you are unemployed.
  5. Take distributions if you are permanently disabled.

Age 59½ and Older

During this time period, you have considerable discretion in determining the dollar amount of distributions that you will take. If you made tax-deductible (tax-deferred) contributions to your retirement plan, you can take distributions in either of two ways:

1. *The "any dollar amount at any time" method:* Take out any dollar amount you wish whenever you want.
2. *The "lump-sum" method:* Take out the entire balance in your retirement account all at once.

Either way, you are required to pay any and all income tax due on the dollar amount of any distributions you receive in any given tax year—unless "10-year averaging" applies to the lump sum. However, if you made nondeductible (after-tax) contributions to your retirement plan, you can take distributions in any amount at any time and owe no income taxes on these distributions.

Required Minimum Distribution (RMD)

If the sum-total balance of all the account holder's retirement accounts has not been distributed by the account holder's 70½ birthday, the following optional allowed distribution methods apply:

1. If you're still working and you have an employer-sponsored plan (such as a defined contribution or a defined benefit retirement plan), you can wait until you actually retire before you are required to take required minimum distributions (RMDs). If you have IRA-based retirement plans (excluding a Roth IRA), you must start taking required minimum distributions as soon as you reach age 70½.
2. If you're not still working, you must take required minimum distributions as soon as you reach age 70½.

Other Features

Several additional features apply to Solo-DB plans.

Administration

The third-party record keeper for the Solo-DB plan provides the signature-ready plan document, calculates the ongoing annual actuarial numbers, prepares all tax forms, and answers any administrative questions that you may have.

Loans

Loans are available if you select this feature, but taking a loan could potentially impact the calculated contribution amount. The plan does not permit hardship withdrawals.

More Than One Plan

You can establish a Solo-DB plan and terminate your existing profit-sharing plan. However, if you have already made your profit-sharing contributions for the current plan year, those contributions might not be deductible if the defined benefit plan is established for the same year.

Rollover

You may roll over and consolidate your other retirement funds into a Solo-DB plan, without dollar-limit pretax contributions.

A Solo-DB individual defined benefit retirement plan allows you to contribute up to $170,000 annually to your retirement plan. It is designed to offer specific dollar benefits to the account owner at retirement.

Keogh Defined Benefit Retirement Plan

STRATEGY 155

**Set up and fund a Keogh defined benefit retirement plan if
you are self-employed and want to provide specific dollar benefits
at retirement.**

The Keogh defined benefit retirement plan is designed to offer specific dollar benefits to the account owner at retirement. It's a qualified retirement plan in which you set a target monthly or annual dollar benefit that you want to receive when you retire. It was designed for self-employed individuals who function as both the employer and an employee; therefore, for purposes of a Keogh, the term *employee* includes a self-employed individual who has earned income. In other words, an owner-employee is both an employer and an employee.

If you are a member of a company retirement plan, you may also set up a Keogh plan for your self-employment side business. For example, if you are an employee of a company that has a qualified 401(k) plan to which you make salary deferrals, you may also set up a Keogh defined benefit retirement plan based on your self-employment earned income.

A Keogh defined benefit retirement provides tax-deductible contributions and tax-free income accumulation (growth) until withdrawn. Remember, in a Keogh defined benefit retirement plan, the employee is not allowed to make any contributions; all contributions are made by the employer on behalf of all eligible employees.

Setup

You may set up your own Keogh defined benefit retirement plan and contribute to it without advance approval; however, advance approval is advisable, and you may ask the IRS, in a determination letter, to review the plan. Approval requirements depend on whether you set up your own plan or join a master plan administered by a bank, an insurance company, a mutual fund, or a prototype plan sponsored by a trade or professional association. If you start our own individually designed plan, you'll need to apply for a determination letter on Form 5300.

You must formally set up a defined benefit Keogh plan before the end of the tax year in which you want the plan to be effective. Contributions are due by the due date of the business's income tax return (including extensions). Excess contributions may be carried over and deducted in later years, subject to the ceiling for those years. However, excess contributions are generally subject to a 10 percent penalty on nondeductible contributions that are not returned by the end of the tax year.

Creating Earned Income (Compensation)

STRATEGY 156

Consider the unique earned income qualification requirements under a Keogh defined benefit retirement plan.

Unlike other retirement plans, a Keogh defined benefit retirement plan does not recognize W-2 wages paid to owner as earned income. This means these W-2 wages cannot be used to qualify you to make contributions to your Keogh. For Keogh plans, earned income is generated only by the sources in Table 22.1, depending on your form of business organization.

Contributions

STRATEGY 157

Make contributions to your Keogh defined benefit retirement plan using contributions from your profit-sharing plan, your money purchase plan, or a paired plan (a combination of profit-sharing and money purchase) up to $42,000 annually.

Contributions are due by the due date of the business's income tax return (including extensions), and are tax deductible to the business. You are required to contribute to your employees' accounts *even if you do not have profits.* Additionally, you are not allowed to make contributions for yourself or an employee if past age 70½.

The maximum contribution that can be made to a defined benefit Keogh retirement plan is the lesser of (1) 100 percent of the employee's compensation up to $210,000 or (2) $42,000. This total contribution can be made in one of three ways: (1) a profit-sharing contribution, plus (2) a money purchase contribution, the total of which, (1) plus (2), may not exceed the lesser of 100 percent of compensation up to $210,000, or $42,000 annually, or (3) a paired contribution, which is a combination of (1) and (2):

Table 22.1   Sources That Qualify as Earned Income for Keogh Plans

Sole Proprietorship
- Bottom-line profit

One-Member LLC
- Taxed as a sole proprietorship: Bottom-line profit

Partnership*
- Pro rata share of bottom-line profit
- Guaranteed payments (even if partnership doesn't make any profit)

Limited Partnership
- General partner
   Pro rata share of bottom-line profit
   Guaranteed payments (even if partnership doesn't make any profit)

- Limited partner(s): Guaranteed payments (even if partnership doesn't make any profit)

Multiple-Member LLC†
- Taxed as a sole partnership: Pro rata share of bottom-line profit

*Partnership plans: An individual partner or partners, although self-employed, may not set up a Keogh plan; the Keogh plan must be established by the partnership. Partnership deductions for contributions to an individual partner's account are reported on the partner's Schedule K-1 (Form 1065) and deducted by the partner as an adjustment to income on line 29 of his or her own individual tax return (Form 1040).
†Members of a multiple-owner LLC, although self-employed, may not set up a Keogh plan; the Keogh plan must be established by the LLC. LLC deductions for contributions to an individual partner's account are reported on the member's Schedule K-1 (Form 1065) and deducted by the member as an adjustment to income on line 29 of his or her own individual tax return (Form 1040).

1. *Profit-sharing plan.* Contributions to the plan are contingent on your business having profit from which to pay the contributions. You can contribute up to 20 percent of your earnings from self-employment, up to a maximum of $42,000 per year. A profit-sharing plan does allow the use of vesting schedules and Social Security integration (not allowed by SEP IRA plans), and you don't have to make a contribution every year.
2. *Money purchase plan.* A plan that requires fixed contributions regardless of your business profits—even if you have a loss. You can contribute more to these plans

than you can to either a profit-sharing plan or a SEP IRA. As an owner, you can contribute the lesser of 100 percent of your self-employment income or $42,000 per year. This allows for a larger contribution; however, *no* flexibility is allowed on the percentage of contributions you make each year. This feature makes this plan better suited for high-income earners who are comfortable enough financially to know they can continue making large-percentage contributions.

Note that the maximum deduction percentage for regular employees under a Keogh defined contribution money purchase plan is 25 percent of their wages.

3. *Paired plans.* A plan that combines the profit-sharing plan and the money purchase plan. You can attain the maximum contribution possible (100 percent) that you can get (as an owner) with the money purchase pension plan, but you have some of the flexibility that comes with a profit-sharing plan. For example, you can fix your money purchase pension plan contributions at 80 percent and contribute anywhere from 0 to 20 percent of your net income to your profit-sharing plan. Thus, in any given plan year, you may contribute as little as 0 percent of your net income or as much as 20 percent.

The Keogh defined benefit retirement plan may prove costly if you have older employees who must be provided with proportionate defined benefits. No employee contributions are allowed; all contributions must be made by the employer.

The Keogh defined benefit retirement plan is for individuals who are able and willing to contribute significant dollar amounts annually to a retirement plan. The exact amount you may contribute will depend on the results of actuarial analysis for each individual employee.

The maximum contribution that can be made to a defined benefit Keogh retirement plan is calculated actuarially in a manner to create a plan that has an adequate amount of dollars (at the time of your retirement) to pay a specific (defined) annual benefit to you during your retirement.

Business Eligibility

STRATEGY 158

Make your business eligible to have a Keogh defined benefit retirement plan for your employees.

You may make your business eligible for Keogh defined benefit retirement plan participation by setting up the plan and contributing to it without any advance approval. However, since advanced approval is advisable, you may, in your determination letter, ask the IRS to review your plan. Approval requirements depend on whether or not you set up your own administered plan or join a master plan administered by a bank, an insurance company, a mutual fund, or a prototype plan sponsored by a trade or professional association. If you start your own individually designed plan, you may apply for a determination letter on Form 5300 (whether the plan is defined benefit or defined contribution). You must pay a fee to the IRS when you apply for a determination letter. File Form 8717, showing your fee, along with Form 5300.

Employee Eligibility (Inclusion)

STRATEGY 159

Apply the inclusion rules for making your employees eligible for participation in your Keogh defined benefit retirement plan.

In order for your employees to be eligible to participate in a Keogh defined benefit retirement plan, your plan must meet the following conditions:

- You must include in your plan all employees who have reached age 21 and who have at least one year of service. An employee may be required to complete two years of service before participating in your plan if your plan provides for full membership and immediate vesting after no more than two years. Note that you are generally not required to cover seasonal or part-time employees who work less than 1000 hours during 12-month period.
- You may not exclude employees who are over a certain age.
- You may not discriminate in favor of officers or other highly compensated personnel.
- You must provide benefits for the employees and their beneficiaries, and their plan rights may not be subject to forfeiture.
- You may not allow any of the funds to be diverted for purposes other than pension benefits.
- You may not receive contributions made on your behalf that exceed the ratio of contributions made on behalf of employees.

Top-Heavy Rules

STRATEGY 160

**Incorporate the IRS top-heavy rules when making contributions
under a Keogh defined benefit retirement plan.**

The top-heavy rules apply if more than 60 percent of a Keogh defined benefit plan account balances, or more than 60 percent of the accrued benefits, are for key employees. These include employees who at any time during the plan year own one of the 10 largest ownership interests and have annual compensation exceeding $30,000 *or* have more than a 5 percent interest in the company *or* have more than a 1 percent interest and also receive annual compensation of more than $150,000.

Officers are considered key employees if they receive annual compensation exceeding $65,000, and key employee treatment is also applicable to employees who were key employees in any of the four preceding years under the applicable compensation limit for each such year.

Even if your pension or profit-sharing plans are not currently considered top-heavy, your plans may be disqualified unless they include provisions that would automatically take effect if the plans were to become top-heavy. The major top-heavy restriction requires an accelerated vesting schedule.

A top-heavy plan must provide either 100 percent vesting after three years of service *or* graded vesting at the rate of at least 20 percent after two years of service, 40 percent after three years of service, 60 percent after four years of service, 80 percent after five years of service, and 100 percent after six years of service. (The "100 percent vesting after three years of service" may be a better option if your business has a high turnover rate.)

The first $170,000 of a self-employed person's earned income is used to determine whether the plan is top-heavy.

Distributions

The methods available for you to take distributions out of your Keogh defined benefit retirement plan depend on your age and other circumstances.

Under Age 59½

You can take distributions out of your Keogh defined benefit retirement plan if you are under age 59½ using the following methods:

1. Take distributions as part of a "series of substantially equal periodic payments" over the life expectancy of the retirement account owner, or life expectancies of the owner and the beneficiary, using one of the following annuity-type methods:
    a. An annuity purchased by your employer
    b. The "fixed amortization method"
    c. The "fixed annuitization method"

    Provided:

    a. The account owner has have left the company during or after the calendar year in which you reached age 55.
    b. The account owner has incurred "separation of service" from the employer (has left the company); however, the account owner may still be employed elsewhere.
    c. The "series of substantially equal periodic payments" continues for a minimum of five years, or until the account owner becomes age 59½.
2. Do a rollover into another retirement account.
3. Pay medical expenses in excess of 7.5 percent of your adjusted gross income (AGI).
4. Pay your health insurance if you are unemployed.
5. Take distributions if you are permanently disabled.

Age 59½ and Older

During this time period, you have considerable discretion in determining the dollar amount of distributions that you will take.

If you made tax-deductible (tax-deferred) contributions to your retirement plan, you can take distributions in either of two ways:

1. *The "any dollar amount at any time" method:* Take out any dollar amount you wish whenever you want.
2. *The "lump-sum" method:* Take out the entire balance in your retirement account all at once.

Either way, you are required to pay any and all income tax due on the dollar amount of any distributions you receive in any given tax year—unless "10-year averaging" applies to the lump sum. However, if you made nondeductible (after-tax) contributions to your retirement plan, you can take distributions in any amount at any time and owe no income taxes on these distributions.

Required Minimum Distribution (RMD)

If the sum-total balance of all the account holder's retirement accounts has not been distributed by the account holder's 70½ birthday, the following optional allowed distribution methods apply:

1. If you're still working and you have an employer-sponsored plan, you can wait until you actually retire before you are required to take required minimum distributions (RMDs). If you have IRA-based retirement plans (excluding a Roth IRA), you must start taking required minimum distributions as soon as you reach age 70½.
2. If you're not still working, you must take required minimum distributions as soon as you reach age 70½.

Other Features

The following additional features are applicable to Keogh defined benefit plans.

Administration

STRATEGY 161

File your Keogh defined benefit plan annual return on or before July 31 of the year following the plan tax year.

The annual Keogh defined benefit plan return is due on July 31 of the year following the plan tax year (unless an extension is obtained from the IRS). Use Form 5500-EZ for one-participant plans (including yourself and your spouse if you are a sole proprietorship or a one-person LLC, or if you and your business partners/members and spouses are operating as either a partnership or a multiple-member LLC in which the only plan participants are partners/members and their spouses). You must file a Form 5500-EZ for the first year the assets of your plan exceed $100,000 and for each year thereafter, even if the plan's total assets drop below the $100,000 threshold (temporarily or permanently).

If you cannot file Form 5500-EZ, you must file Form 5500-C/R if there are fewer than 100 plan participants (Form 5500 if there are 100 or more participants).

Controlled Groups

STRATEGY 162

Aggregate your Keogh defined benefit contributions from more than one business to avoid violating the "controlled group" limitations.

Multiple businesses owned by the same individual(s) are called a *controlled group;* under these circumstances, the businesses are aggregated for purposes of the limitation applied to defined benefits. If you have more than one business, you cannot set up separate Keogh defined benefit accounts to avoid the applicable annual dollar limits on contributions.

Vesting

Keogh defined benefit retirement plans allow vesting schedules, which require employees to remain with the business for a specified number of years before they earn the right to their full retirement account balances. *Vesting* refers to the portion of the retirement account dollars that the employer owns. After a certain number of years, employees become "fully vested" and therefore own 100 percent of their share of the funds. If an employee leaves prior to becoming fully vested, he or she loses the unvested balance, which reverts to the remaining plan participants on a pro rata basis.

Loans

Owner-employee Keogh defined benefit plan loans to an owner-employee (more than 10 percent ownership) are subject to prohibited-transaction penalties. There are two penalties:

1. A 15 percent first-tier penalty
2. A 100 percent penalty

The 15 percent penalty applies to the year of the loan and later years until the loan is repaid with interest. The penalty is figured on a fair-market interest factor. The 100 percent penalty is imposed if the loan is not repaid. The penalty may be avoided by repaying the loan within 90 days after the IRS sends a deficiency notice for the 100 percent tax. If you are an owner-employee, you may be able to apply to the Department of Labor for a special exemption from the prohibited-transaction penalties.

Prohibitions

The following restrictions apply to Keogh defined benefit plans:

- They cannot be converted to Roth.
- They cannot be self-directed.
- Nondeductible contributions are not allowed.
- Note: Owner can have more than one business, but only one business can have a Keogh plan.

A Keogh defined benefit retirement plan allows contributions in three ways: (1) profit sharing, (2) money purchase, or (3) a paired plan, combining the two, up to $42,000 annually.

Index

About the Author

David W. Meier has always been an entrepreneur at heart, starting with the proverbial Kool-Aid stand, door-to-door sales, yard mowing, newspaper delivery, his own rock 'n' roll band playing his way through college, and starting and building a successful chain of retail musical record and tape stores. This hands-on experience gave him a unique insight into the world of small-business entrepreneurship at a very young age.

After completing his formal education, a BA in economics from the University of Michigan and an MBA from Loyola of Baltimore, Mr. Meier spent much of the 1970s teaching finance, accounting, and tax courses at local community colleges, at the University of Maryland, and at George Mason University.

In the early 1980s, he created an accounting and tax consulting group specifically dedicated to helping small-business owners become more successful. During the past two decades, Mr. Meier has traveled throughout this country presenting small-business seminars and workshops to thousands of would-be, new, and existing small-business owners.

With creation of The Small Business Advantage, a company providing personal business coaching to small-business owners, and the *Make Your Life Tax Deductible* book, Mr. Meier is realizing a lifelong dream of providing thousands more individuals with the knowledge and ongoing support required to help them become truly successful entrepreneurs!

For additional assistance with your new business idea or your existing small business, go to www.thesmallbusinessadvantage.com.